Institutional Web Presence in Agriculture

About the Authors

Amrita Bhattacharyya has completed her M.Sc (Ag.) in Agricultural Extension from the Department of Agricultural Extension, Palli Siksha Bhavana (Institute of Agriculture), Visva-Bharati, Sriniketan. Currently, she works for the Indian postal service in West Bengal.

Darshan N.P. has been working as an assistant professional in the Department of Agricultural Extension Palli Siksha Bhavana (Institute of Agriculture), Visva-Bharati, Sriniketan, since December 2020. He completed his B.Sc in Agriculture from UAS, Bengaluru, M.Sc in Agricultural Extension Education from ICAR-NDRI, Karnal and Ph.D in Agricultural Extension from PJTSAU, Hyderabad. His field of work includes Organisation development, Communication, and Agricultural Psychology.

Institutional Web Presence in Agriculture

Amrita Bhattacharyya
M.Sc (Ag.) Agricultural Extension
Palli Siksha Bhavana, Visva-Bharati (A Central University)
Sriniketan-731236, West Bengal

Darshan N.P.
Assistant Professor
Department of Agricultural Extension
Palli Siksha Bhavana, Visva-Bharati (A Central University)
Sriniketan-731236, West Bengal

PMW

PMW
FU 75, Pitam Pura
New Delhi 110034
publishmywork23@gmail.com
Mob. 91-8447075807

Print ISBN: 978-93-61345-58-6

ebook ISBN: 978-93-61347-48-1

Dr. (Ms.) Anindita Saha
Associate Professor & Head
Department of Agricultural Extension, PSB
Visva-Bharati

Foreword

Websites are serving as invaluable tools for education and information dissemination within the agricultural sector, facilitating the exchange of knowledge among diverse stakeholders. Websites provide a platform for agricultural agencies and institutions to share research findings, training materials, and extension services, empowering practitioners to make informed decisions and improve productivity. These platforms become central hubs for farmers, educators, and students to access relevant and timely information, keeping them abreast of the latest developments in the field. However, to maximize the impact of these platforms, it's essential to design websites that prioritize fast access to accurate and relevant information, catering to the specific needs of users.

Considering these aspects, the authors have timely penned this book titled "Institutional Web Presence in Agriculture: Status, Approach and Case Study", which explores the significance of institutional websites in contributing to the ever-changing nexus of information, communication, and technology for agricultural development.

By examining the status, strategic approaches, and real-world case studies, the authors provide invaluable insights into harnessing the full potential of institutional web presence. The insights and recommendations of the book pave the way for a more connected, informed, and resilient agricultural ecosystem, ensuring the sustainable development of all stakeholders involved.

I appreciate the authors for their meticulous research, insightful analysis, and unwavering commitment to advancing the agricultural sector through digital innovation.

Anindita Saha
29.03.2024

Dr. (Ms.) Anindita Saha

Preface

Agricultural Extension Education is progressively harnessing internet-supported ICT systems to deliver services to farming communities. Institutional websites have evolved into pivotal sources of information for academic, research, and advisory purposes. These platforms not only proclaim the presence of individuals, research groups, institutions, and departments but also serve to publicize their accomplishments. Moreover, they facilitate the distribution of research findings through the publication of summaries, datasets, tools, and web articles. The potential benefits of maintaining a robust web presence extend beyond academia, impacting research visibility, student recruitment, media interest, and business collaborations. To assess the effectiveness of institutional websites, a methodology known as Webometrics is employed, involving the study of all network-based communications using informetric or other quantitative measures. In the context of a pluralistic extension scenario, it is imperative to analyze and compare the competitive ecosystem among institutional websites. Hence, this book, based on empirical research, uniquely explores institutional web presence viz-a-viz, content domain, delivery mechanisms, multimodal services, and stakeholder coverage.

This book identifies parameters crucial for delivering agricultural advisory services through institutional websites.

Authors

Preface

Contents

1

Introduction

The agriculture sector in India accounts for about 20.2 per cent of its gross value added (GVA) and 17.34 per cent of the total export earnings. It employs approximately 60 per cent of the country's workforce. It is an unavoidable source for generating demand for industrial goods and services, and domestic savings in rural India are a huge source of resource mobilization in the Indian economy. This sector plays a key role in ensuring national food security and, in the meantime, national security as well. For these reasons, the development of agriculture has a strong multiplier effect on the economy. There is also an increasing consensus that a globalizing economy and a long-term economic development plan for India are practicable only if it has agriculture and raises rural incomes as its central concern.

ICT and Information Needs of the Stakeholders

Information and communications technology (ICT) is an extension-related term used in information technology (IT) that emphasizes the role of unified communications and the integration of telecommunications like wireless signals and telephone systems and computers; it is also useful in the software system, middleware, storage, and audio-visual, that enable users to store, transmit, access, manipulate information by understanding the whole process.

ICT is also called the union of audio-visual and telephone systems with computer networks through a single cabling or link system. Various economic inducements exist to merge the telephone network with the computer systems. ICT is an umbrella term; it includes communication devices, including radio, television, telephones, computers, network hardware, satellites, and so on, as well as various services and appliances such as video conference and distance learning. ICT also includes analogue technologies, like paper communication and other modes that help transmit communication.

The concepts of ICTs are always evolving. It indicates a product that will retrieve, manipulate, store, receive, transmit and receive information electronically in a digital mode, like personal computers, including digital television, mobile phones, and robots. Skills Framework for the Information Age is one of many models to describe and manage competencies for ICT professionals in this 22nd century.

ICT is an information-handling tool with equipment, services, and applications used to store, produce, process, distribute and exchange information. It is also an electronically interactive bridge between Farmers and Extension Workers.

There are different types of ICT tools like –

1. Traditional tools
   - Radio
   - Television
   - Print Media
2. Modern tools
   - Internet
   - Multimedia
   - Mobile
   - Audio conference
   - Video conference
   - Social Networking tools

ICT mainly manages external stakeholders through simulation, social media, and visualization. Taking a socio-materiality lens, we can demonstrate how these practices are used for diverse programs to manage external stakeholders. Anchored in directions of a powerful framework, we can discuss how these ICT practices can be strategically used for framing, persuading, and hegemonizing the external stakeholders in megaprojects. Theoretically, the roles of ICT can be highlighted for managing external stakeholders in case of the current use of improving the advantage of internal stakeholders. Social media is generally used in articulating practices in all strategic roles, maintaining it as a critical ICT tool to manage external stakeholder management in infrastructure.

According to many studies, ICTs have aided farmers in adopting new technologies, such as new varieties, and accessing the market and other crucial information. The extension system gradually shifted to ICTs to transmit adequately packaged agricultural information to farmers to boost agricultural productivity. As a result, the study will determine how effective ICTs are in access. As a result, the success of ICTs will aid the extension system inappropriately utilizing them to provide agricultural information to farmers. It can also instruct extension workers on which ICTs to employ or how to combine them.

Extension must use ICT systems to deliver farm information to farmers to keep up with the fast-paced pace of digital technology. ICTs have been used in India's farming sector for a few years. However, it must be seen how far farming and communities are willing to go to use ICTs to improve their farming. Furthermore, it is a question of whether ICTs and the information they send are valuable, proper, and appropriate. The answers to these questions will undoubtedly provide a foundation for policymakers and planners to integrate extension communication through ICTs for training sector reform.

Websites for Information Dissemination

Web portals are generally used to form coordination among the communities of actors by disseminating and pooling knowledge like centralizing data of sub-basin management plans and on environmental contracts, news publications related to the management of water, newsletters, and provision of documents; apart from that sharing, gathering and highlighting experiences in the records, forums and themed sections; and supporting actors to build skills in dissemination of studies and guides, organization of web-conferences.

Website portals generally adopt design responsiveness principles, offering visitors a comfortable consultation irrespective of the medium used (mobile phone, tablet, or computer). Unified with an efficient search engine, it helps to make the resources much easier. The addition of interactive maps also helps share experiences, information, and geographical searches for local and international actions depending on the case.

The quality and effectiveness of extension services are critical to the agricultural sector's long-term viability and output. Farmers have been getting agricultural information from extension workers via interpersonal communication for many years. Still, the number of extension employees has been declining while the number of farming families has increased. As a result, the country's current extension service needs to improve in reaching out to farmers with timely and relevant agricultural information. ICTs are considered a partial answer to quickly getting information to the growing number of farming households because relevant and timely information is vital in agriculture. Farmers may receive up-to-date knowledge and information on agricultural technologies, best practices, markets, price patterns, and customer preferences through its use.

Since farmers in many parts of India, including West Bengal, are becoming more mobile and internet savvy, disseminating useful real-time information about crops, soils, climate, cultivation practices, financing, produce storage, and marketing to farming communities is more important and challenging. Many concerted efforts from the government, non-government organizations, and industry are now required to make our farmers ICT-friendly so that the benefits of rapidly evolving technological advancements in farm production, storage, and marketing can be shared equally among all communities and sectors of farming.

Institutional websites have become one of the most important sources of information for academic and research purposes. Regarding research, educational institutions' websites can proclaim the presence of individuals, research groups, institutions, and departments and publicize their accomplishments. They can also distribute discoveries by publishing summaries, data sets, tools, or hosting web articles. The pages can be made centrally by administrators or web admins or logically by people for their own or research team initiatives. More significant research impact, attracting students, media interest, and business contacts are all potential benefits of having a strong web presence. In this context, it seems sensible to investigate measures of website effectiveness, both to learn more about the communication activity they represent and to develop helpful evaluation metrics. As a result of the privatization of education, it is vital to rate educational institution websites in the context of competition among them. Webometrics is the name given to the method, which entails studying all network-based communications using informetric or other quantitative measures. The use of informetric technologies such as word counts and other comparable techniques to the WWW is evident.

According to a literature review, many studies in foreign nations have been conducted on various aspects of website analysis, such as link structure analysis, which involves the examination of Self Links, Hyperlinks, External Links, Inlinks, and Co-Links. Web Impact Factor, search engine performance, webpage content analysis, and web usage analysis have all been studied.

Given the importance of websites for knowledge management, it is critical to assess how accessible and useful these websites are for the stakeholders to advance farming. In the webometric research in India, only a few studies were found. Addressing the following research questions becomes important to analyze agriculture and allied websites.

Research Questions

RQ-1: How many websites are related to the Agriculture and allied sectors?

RQ-2: What content is offered by websites related to Agriculture and allied sectors?

RQ-3: What is the web usage pattern of websites related to Agriculture and allied sectors?

The answers to these questions were analyzed through the following objectives.

Objective

1. To explore websites related to Agriculture and allied sectors in West Bengal.
2. To study the webpage content analysis of websites related to agricultural and allied sectors.
3. To analyze the web usage pattern of websites related to agricultural and allied sectors.

The study of webometric content analysis is important for effective knowledge management. The present study revealed the number of websites associated with agricultural and allied sectors in West Bengal, their page contents, and their usage pattern. Exploring the number of websites would help understand the status of the tech-savviness of farming stakeholders. Analyzing the webpage contents would provide the content base of the websites, and identifying the usage pattern would help to understand the information domain of the websites. This study also gives suggestions to institutions, organizations, policymakers, line department personnel, and researchers to plan for future courses of action for the effective constitution and organization of websites for knowledge management in West Bengal and other similar regions of the country.

2

Literature and Citations

A literature review attempts to discover, locate, and synthesize relevant research reports, articles, books, and other resources relating to a study subject. The review can be based on published sources like journal articles, conference papers, research abstracts, chapter books, research institution websites , and so on, as well as unpublished materials like theses and dissertations. By examining the literature, a researcher can take advantage of past research and results made by professionals to get the most out of their research.

Examining literature is an important part of every research project since it gives the investigator the information, they need to frame the study on the chosen topic. It directs an investigation on the appropriate path, keeping up with the most recent data.

Studies on Broad Areas of Webometrics

Webometric studies, ranging from earlier to more contemporary studies, have been recognized and organized under the following headings:

- Studies on the Growth and Development of Webometrics
- Studies on theoretical studies of content analysis
- Studies on Web Content Analysis
- Studies on web usage analysis
- Nature and Extent of use of ICTs by the farming community.
- Nature of farmers' perception about the appropriateness, usefulness, and constraints of using ICTs in farming.
- Studies on web usage analysis

Studies on the Growth and Development of Webometrics

Bossy (1995) investigated the impact of the INTERNET on scientific communities and, as a result, on Scientometrics. Until now, scientometrics has not studied internet-mediated scientific interaction systematically.

Larson (1996) conducted an exploratory investigation of 30 terabytes of web pages collected by the Inktomi "Web Crawler" and the usage of the DEC AltaVista search engine for co-citation analysis of a group of Earth Science relevant internet sites using the DEC AltaVista search engine. The statistical properties of web documents and their hypertext linkages are analyzed, and the characteristics of highly cited web documents are evaluated.

Webometrics, or the application of informetric methods to the World Wide Web (WWW), was first introduced by Almind and Ingwersen (1997). This case study demonstrates a practical way of calculating informetric analysis parameters in general. According to the findings, Denmark lags behind other Nordic countries regarding online visibility and its place in scientific databases.

Webometrics as a methodology for the World Wide Web was investigated by Moses, Beatrice, and Philippos (1999). They first introduced the technique and demonstrated how it might be applied, then utilized the European and global information societies as examples to demonstrate webometrics methodology.

Owen (2000) presented a webometric analysis of the connections (or citations) to websites linked with the Departments of Librarianship and Information Science. Some of the observed citation counts appear counter-intuitive, and there is some evidence to support this.

Bjorneborn and Ingwersen (2001) highlight selected webometric research areas, as well as recent search engine coverage and performance investigations, as a framework for choosing quality and content analysis . Web Impact Factors (Web-IF) measurement issues are examined. According to the authors, new paths in webometrics are given for performing knowledge discovery and issue tracking on the Web, partly based on bibliometric methodologies employed in bibliographic and citation databases.

According to AltaVista, Thelwal et al. (2002) report on the findings of a survey of the sizes of 670 websites of higher education institutions in nations linked with the European Union. It discovers that huge country variations of up to three orders of magnitude still exist.

Three new metrics have been introduced by Thelwall and Wilkinson (2003) that measure the range of use of a university website by its peers through different heuristics for counting links targeted at its pages. All three give results that correlate significantly with the research productivity of the target institution. The directory range model, which is based on summing the number of distinct directories targeted by each other university, produces the most promising results of any link metric yet. Based upon an analysis of changes between models, it is suggested that range models measure essentially the same quantity as their predecessors but are less susceptible to spurious causes of multiple links and are more robust.

Webometrics is a field that combines contributions from information science, computer science, and statistics to analyze web phenomena quantitatively, according to Thelwall and Vaughan's (2004) statistical physics. Its methodology is heavily influenced by bibliometrics.

Webometrics was described by Bjorneborn and Ingwersen (2004) as a subfield of informetric studies and bibliometrics that belongs to library and information science and is related to cybernetics as a generic subfield. When applying the provided conceptual framework, they produced a consistent and precise link typology and nomenclature and made apparent the contrast between different Web node levels.

According to Malgeri, Longheu, and Carchiolo (2005), the lack of clear structure in web documents makes it difficult to understand data semantics; therefore, comprehension of the logical organization of web data relies on the user's perception of the underlying author's schema. In this study, they describe a web structuring strategy based on analyzing the structure and semantics of both web pages and sites to uncover and give users hidden schemas.

Cheng-Zhi (2005) claims that traditional website evaluation criteria are extensively used to evaluate online content, an important component of information literacy instruction in academic institutions. A more informed assessment requires webometric evaluation standards that use measurable data and physical information. While traditional criteria remain convenient and beneficial, particularly for new web users, the author suggests that simple webometric criteria can provide further insights into evaluating online resources.

The reasons for the emergence of informetrics were examined by Egghe (2006). (bibliometrics, Scientometrics, webometrics). Two special Information Processing and Management issues have been dedicated to "Informetrics." They engaged with models and science mapping (co-citation, analysis), websites and search engines, digital library collaboration, and the newest area in informetrics: the use of and access to articles in digital libraries.

According to Ingwersen (2006), webometrics has grown substantially in the last ten years; not only is the phrase used more frequently, but there are more publications and even monographs on the subject, and at least one professor has been appointed in the field.

In the in-laws of Webometrics , Alimohammadi (2006) developed a link between bibliometrics and webometrics . As a result, Lotka's law might be applied to webometrics as the number of webliographies creating webliographies. Bradford's law tends to three parts, as a core of webliographies on the issue, which produced one-third of all websites while being very few. Even though the second zone had the same number of websites as the first, it had more webliographies.

Pinto et al. (2007) reviewed the Spanish public university websites dedicated to the European Higher Education Area (EHEA). Visibility, authority, updates, accessibility, correctness and completeness, quality assessment, and navigability were employed in their analysis.

Webometrics , a modern, fast-growing offshoot of bibliometrics, has been examined in detail by Thelwall (2008), who compares early bibliometrics with current practice and outlines a range of recent advancements.

The trends from bibliometrics to webometrics were traced by Samir, Subal, and Mukhopadhyay (2009). Some key application areas of webometrics study, the methods used for data collecting, web analytic methodologies and tools, and issues encountered in web research have all been covered. This article presents webometric research of 13 Indian Institutes of Technology (IITs) and Indian Institutes of Management (IIMs).

Because discovering free scholarly EJs, especially medical ones, is difficult in the web environment, Isfandyari-Moghaddam, Danesh, and HadjiAzizi (2015) investigated the most accredited free English electronic journals (EJs) in Medical Sciences. The most reputable publications in the four medical disciplines examined are Nursing: Online Journal of Rural Nursing and Health Care and Online Journal of Nursing Informatics; New South Wales Public Health Bulletin, PLoS Biology, and Environmental Health Perspectives – National Institute of Environmental Health Sciences.

The qualitative content analysis conducted by Ninkov and Vaughan (2017) verified this finding. The research provides techniques to disseminate professional information more successfully on the Internet . The research shows that webometrics analysis may be used to investigate online information dissemination. This type of analysis can be used to investigate health and other data.

Theoretical Studies on Content Analysis

Speed asked, "Do newspapers currently convey the news?" in the first quantitative newspaper analysis 1893. Between 1881 and 1891, the author of the newspaper disclosed that New York newspapers covered fewer religious, scientific, and literacy issues in favour of favour, sports, and scandals.

Max Weber (1911) advocated a large-scale content study of the press at the German Sociological Society's first conference in 1910, but it did not work for various reasons.

At the same time, Andrei Markov (1913) was working on a theory of symbol chains, and he published a statistical study of a sample of Pushkin's tale in verse, 'Eugene Onegin.' These inquiries were recently found and only had a minor impact on the content analysis literature.

Janis (1943) excluded pragmatic content analysis because causes or consequences of content can only be validated in rare cases purely by analyzing the messages, according to Janis (1943). In the broadest sense, content data is used in conjunction with independent behavioural indicators, either directly or indirectly.

Berelson and Lazarsfeld (1948) published the first concise presentation of the conceptual and methodological developments separately under the new umbrella of content analysis in a mimeographed text titled "The Analysis of Communication Content," which was later published as Berenson's Content Analysis in Communication Research (1952).

According to Berelson (1952), content analysis is a research approach for objectively, systematically, and quantitatively describing the manifest content of communication. It is less restrictive, according to Berelson (1952), and comprises research in which conclusions are expressed using phrases like "more," "less," or "growing."

According to Berelson (1952), content analysis is useful for analyzing content's features, causes, and effects.

Sebeok and Zeps (1958) described the first computer-assisted content analysis, using rudimentary information retrieval algorithms to analyze roughly 4000 Cheremis folktales.

According to George (1959), qualitative examination of a set number of critical communications yields more information about a speaker's specific objectives at a given time than more conventional procedures. Qualitative content analysis , defined as making conclusions based on the presence or absence of qualities in communications, has been justified primarily, but not only, for its superior performance in practical social science problems.

According to Stone, the participants at the 1947 Workshop on Content Analysis in the Social Sciences in Pisa, Italy, considered the development of adequate algorithms for computer content analysis to be the main impediment to better content analysis (1975). Since then, computational methods have evolved in a variety of ways.

The lack of a uniform process and measuring instrument in survey research, according to Namenwrith and Weber (1987), was one of the reasons why content analysis did not function. This worked against the accumulation of similar resources.

There is no one-size-fits-all approach to content analysis , according to Weber (1990). Investigators must choose which strategies are most suited to their specific problems. In addition, several technical issues with content analysis must be addressed or are the topic of current research and debate.

Studies on Web Content Analysis

At Georgia Institute of Technology, Catledge and Pitkow (1995) did a study that collected client-side user events of NCSA's mosaic. Actual user behaviour, as established by client-side log file analysis, added to our understanding of user navigation methods and offered real-world data on interface usage. The log data analysis resulted in design and usability recommendations for web pages, sites, and browsers.

According to Thelwal et al. (2001), most Internet searches begin with a search engine, which uses its organized directory structure or text query facility to find information. Many search engines, including Google, AltaVista, and HotBot, offer Boolean text matching in response to the difficulty in identifying the most relevant pages for some information needs. Others like Google, AltaVista, and HotBot can integrate additional information into a more advanced request.

According to Gopalakrishnan, Ambuja, and Seetharama (2002), the World Wide Web has revolutionized information transfer. The authors investigated the type and pattern of information scientists' citations in Indian seminar proceedings and one volume of an international publication in the library and information science field. According to the findings, the citation pattern has shifted over time, and web citations will eventually replace traditional types of citations.

To augment the current Web Impact Factor, Thelwall (2003) added two web link count measures. The first is interpreted as a measure of a university's average level of online informal scholarly communication and information consumption by academics. The second has a similar layout but focuses on the degree of web interconnectedness in terms of links and outlines. The latter metric is based on a more complex mechanism than raw link counts: it totals the minimum number of university links across all pairs in the chosen set containing the institution.

Jose, Isidro, and Jose (2006) did a longitudinal analysis of the evolution of 738 websites and stated it two times in time (1997 and 2004). The major findings show that web content and elements are growing but also that there is a significant level of web content deterioration. The results imply that the Web is characterized by great dynamism and instability across the seven years studied.

According to Papachristos and Avouris (2011), preference mapping is a collection of multivariate statistical techniques aiming to better understand product preference by considering the heterogeneity of participants. The study's findings demonstrated a strong link between credibility and visual appeal.

Ortega and Aguillo (2011) concentrated on measuring website performance. The main web-based tools and approaches for evaluating the effectiveness of higher education websites were outlined, as well as how those information networks were established and deployed. Broder et al.'s bow-tie model of the Web and Bjornrborn's Corona model were both lectured. The individual and overall indicators like P – cliques, K – Cores, Distance, Diameter, and Global Clustering Coefficient were studied as network indicators. The software created co-link analyses, network graphs of world-class universities, and geographic maps, then discussed by rating.

Sadat-Moosavi and Tajeddini (2012) investigated the accessibility and decay of online resources cited in academic libraries and information science publications in ISI and the Emerald database. It was advised that reviewing online citations before publication, acquiring backups of cited publications, utilizing more stable file formats and domains, and using tools like Web Site and Digital Object Identifier to avoid long URLs would assist in avoiding them.

Millot (2015) discovered that while the techniques of the two forms of rankings have certain similarities, the results of the two types of rankings also tend to converge. Rankings for the system should be more inclusive in terms of the number and types of nations they cover, and they should better reflect the diversity of missions carried out by national governments.

Nature and Extent of use of ICTs by Farming Community

Fischer et al. (2009) argue that information and communication technology (ICT) has enormous potential and should be accorded the same priority as the biotechnology revolution. In India, the influence of mobiles on agricultural information will be determined by how well mobile networks can connect farmers to market information quickly and accurately.

According to A. Aphunu (2011) states that the bulk of the respondents (95 %) had access to radio and telephone (both landline and GSM), while 93.3 per cent had access to television. Access to the Internet , computer-based communication devices, and other technologies were limited among respondents.

This research by Surabhi Mittal et al. (2012) provides evidence of the impact of mobile phones in lowering information search costs and asymmetries and boosting market efficiencies. Poor farmers have benefitted from mobile phones by increasing their market participation and diversification into high-value crops. This move has helped farmers earn more money by increasing price realization and reducing waste.

According to Manoj Sharma et al. (2014), 41 per cent of farmers possessed a landline phone, but only 47 per cent used it for farming. Similarly, while 98 per cent of farmers owned a television, just 49 per cent used it to watch agriculture-related programming. Farmers own more than 98 per cent of mobile phones, which they mostly use for social communication. However, 78% of farmers said they occasionally use their phones for agriculture advisory, such as calling agriculture departments, relatives, or commission agents to inquire about the production rate.

R. Syiem and colleagues (2015) The majority of the farmers had cell phones, television, and radio, according to the findings. Mobile phones were the most used ICT . Farmers used mobile phones extensively for social communication, contacting mediators for crop marketing, and contacting specialists on a real-time basis for agricultural recommendations.

Farmers viewed market information, such as daily updates on the pricing of agricultural commodities in the local markets of the surrounding district, as one of the most important ICT services, according to K. Lokeswari (2016).

Nature of Perception of Farmers About the Appropriateness, Usefulness, and Constraints of Using ICTs in Farming

According to A. E. Agwu et al. (2008) significant barriers to ICT use include a lack of adequately trained computer personnel, a lack of confidence in operating modern ICTs, erratic and fluctuating power supply, poor finance, lack of internet access in rural areas, and the high cost of ICTs hard and software, among others.

According to Anselme B. Adegbidi and colleagues (2012), it is critical to promote ICT tools in rural areas through ICT infrastructure development and training on ICT tool use for farmers, particularly smallholders, to obtain market information.

According to their findings, Adegbidi, Anselme B., and colleagues (2012), to collect market information, it is necessary to promote ICT tools in rural regions through measures such as ICT infrastructure development and training on ICT tool use for farmers, particularly smallholders. The majority of respondents (66.7 %) said technology was less acceptable. As a result, more research may be performed to determine why other information obtained through various ICT methods appears less relevant to farmers. In addition, a lack of energy, basic knowledge of ICTs, availability of ICT services to rural farmers, and lack of training on specific elements are all significant barriers to accessing various ICT services in the study areas.

According to C. O. Albert et al. (2014), the main barriers to ICT adoption were poverty, a lack of resources, and a lack of computer skills and literacy among farmers. It was, therefore, suggested that extension personnel learn how to manipulate all ICT tools efficiently to instruct farmers by establishing zonal internet centres in the villages.

According to Dr P.Sireesha et al. (2014), significant constraints in the use of ICT tools include a lack of technically competent personnel, problems with ICT tool maintenance, interruptions in Internet connectivity, insufficient budget allocation for ICT tools, lack of ICT equipment up-gradation, and the problem of viruses and junk mails.

According to K. H. Kabir's (2015) analysis of farmer perceptions of the appropriateness of the information, most respondents (37.8%) regarded information on different input services and their availability as the most important, while post-harvest technology data was regarded as less important.

Studies on Web Usage Analysis

Nicholas et al. (1999) examined web log analysis's advantages (and drawbacks), demonstrating their findings in appraising The Times and Sunday Times websites . Nearly a million people worldwide have signed up for these sites, and their online behaviours - the new international and information consumers - matter.

Nichola et al. (2000) detailed a study undertaken on The Times/The Sunday Times websites to discover the best methods for analyzing the use and determining what kind of analyses could be produced.

According to Thelwall (2001), web log files are a useful source of information regarding visitor site use, navigation behaviour, and, to a degree, demographics. This study took data from a single web log file to demonstrate its usefulness to the site owner and people who want to learn more about how web users behave online.

Many attempts have been made to investigate the content of the Web, using either human or automatic agents. Thelwall (2002) identified five previously used Web survey approaches, each of which could be justified. He concluded that any scientific endeavour to crawl the Web must make the parameters available so that researchers can, in theory, reproduce tests or be aware of and account for discrepancies in techniques.

The issues of characterizing and comparing the content utilization of digital information services were examined by Nicholas, Huntington, and Homewood (2003), who looked at three digital platforms in the health industry. However, the article's major focus is a comparison of five sources of health data via their log files. A total of two million page views were analyzed, with over 5000 unique health sites included.

Lee and Hong (2005) used three methods to analyze users' current websites : a user satisfaction survey, ii) user segmentation based on user behaviour, and iii) revamping important web pages to differentiate casual characteristics to improve the performance of the targeted groups. Data mining methods were used for the study, and it was decided that data mining tools might be used indefinitely for online intelligence. By regularly and adequately rebuilding key web pages on the website, present all targeted consumers with lower and benefit them with well-designed content to increase those levels.

Lee and Hong (2005) used three methods to analyze users' current websites : a user satisfaction survey, ii) user segmentation based on user behaviour, and iii) revamping important web pages to differentiate casual characteristics to improve the performance of the targeted groups. Data mining methods were used for the study, and it was decided that data mining tools might be used indefinitely for online intelligence. By regularly and adequately rebuilding key web pages on the website, present all targeted consumers with lower and benefit them with well-designed content to increase those levels.

The transaction logs of NAVER, a popular Korean Web search engine, were examined by Park, Lee, and Bae (2005) to follow the information-seeking behaviour of Korean Web users. Over 40 million requests were collected in these transaction logs for a week. This study revealed that consumers operate straightforwardly: they write in short queries with a few query terms, rarely use sophisticated features, and only look at a few pages of results.

Huntington et al. (2006) analyzed log files from the OhioLINK electronic journal service using microanalytical approaches (i.e., the study of short segments and parts of log files). They provided an analysis based on sub-network labels of journal subject groupings and departments and discovered a degree of association between department name and subject.

According to Buzikashvili (2007), a Web query log analysis might be significantly skewed depending on the number of agents (non-human customers) included in the log. The author presented a consistent strategy that would operate equally well for all observation periods. The sliding window technique is used in this method, where a threshold is set to the sliding window rather than the entire observation period.

Metrics produced from user visits or sessions provide a tool for analyzing Websites and an essential insight into online information-seeking behaviour, according to Huntington, Nicholas, and Jamali (2008). Because of the significant disparities in view times between pages, the authors propose that the page time distribution comprises several distinct view time distributions (abstract, contents page, full text).

Kastania and Zimeras (2010) discussed web application of products, consumption and development of document-centric, interactive usability, and Graphic User Interfaces. They used three approaches to categorize the websites : web typology, digital business models, stages of developmental models and the use of a grading system. Each method was broken down into steps and sub-methods. In addition, the usability of online applications was evaluated based on response times, interaction efficiency, colours, text layout, page structure, navigation structure, multiculturalism, and other factors. To assess the usability of a web application, experimental methods, analytic methods, and experimental methods were outlined.

Bowler, Hong, and He (2011) examined the visibility of six health websites to see which ones provided credible health information. The Google Webmaster tool collected links categorized according to the creator type. The study discovered that a weak network of inlinks resulted in missed opportunities for healthcare workers and young people. It was also found that the Google webmaster in the link tool did not guarantee 100 per cent coverage and that certain links were missed.

Iroaganachi, Ilogho, Itsekor, and Osinulu (2016) evaluated the amount of research published and the top ten published universities, fields, journals, impact factors, cited authors, and top ten published nations. This was done to assess the relevance of the authors, institutional priorities, and the amount of sustainable development in the areas and host nations.

3

Concepts and Theory

Websites

Information science is an interdisciplinary field that skirts the study of the organization, production, retrieval, storage, retrieval, use of information, and dissemination. Information and Metric studies of storage and recovery are the primary areas of Information Science. Today's challenges for information personnel are to pave the way through enormous volumes of information brought about by different means.

The World Wide Web (WWW), an information space, is a complex structure that incorporates all types of information that need different users and a layperson to the researcher. It is a system of interlinked hypertext documents approached via the Internet . The web pages can be viewed in a way that contains images, text, videos, and several multimedia through the forms of a web browser and negotiated between them with the help of hyperlinks.

It is also a system of multimedia that supports uniquely formatted, using markup languages like HTML or digital documents. These scripting languages support links to other documents, video files, graphics, and audio.

The term 'Webometrics ' (Bajorneborne & Ingwersen, 2001) was coined for content analysis , search engine performances, quantitative analysis of web-related phenomena, links, and web technology analysis from an information science perspective.

Sometimes referred to as a website or site, it is a set of related web pages covering content such as video, audio, text, images, etc. A website is laid on one web server, approachable via a network such as the private local area network or the network through an Internet address, known as a Uniform Resource Locator (URL). URL consists of a domain name, the IP address, and root path ('/') in an Internet Protocol-based network called Wikipedia. All publicly accessible websites , sometimes with a little constraint like subscription, collectively constitute the WWW . The restrictions were poised to parts of news websites, business sites, journal websites, file-sharing websites, gaming websites, web-based email, social networking sites and websites providing real-time data on the stock market, and websites providing various services (e.g., websites sharing images or files and so forth).

3.1. Structure and Functions of Websites

The website can be accessed from a standard URL called the web address. The URLs of the concerned pages are organized into an organized hierarchy. However, hyperlinking carries the user's perceived site structure and guides the user's navigation, including a home page with most links to the site's web content and another supplementary about, contents and link page.

The WWW is hierarchical in structure. This hierarchy claims its origin as the Domain Name System (DNS). The DNS helps translate an organization's address (e.g. vbu.ac.in) into the corresponding IP address (e.g. 173.16.2.6). As per the structure from the right-hand side, the domain name has the following hierarchy:

- Top-level domain - .in
- Sub-level domain - .ac
- Server / Computer domain -. vbu.

3.1.1 Web Page

A document on the WWW is known as a Web page. A web page documents a resourceful informational system suitable for the WWW. It can be accessed through a browser and displayed on a mobile device or monitor like www.findmehere.com. A web page is a document typically written as text dispersed with some formatting instructions of HyperText Markup Language like (HTML, XHTML). A webpage may insert elements from another website with suitable markup anchors.

WebPages are accessed and transported with the Hypertext Transfer Protocol known as HTTP, which may optionally employ encryption (HTTP et al.) to provide security and privacy for the user of the webpage content. The user's application, especially a web browser, arranges the page content according to its HTML markup instructions according to a display terminal. In their final presentation, web pages usually subsume many other resources, such as scripts, style sheets and images.

The website pages can generally be accessed from a simple URL called a web address. Although hyperlinking between them conveys the reader's perceived site structure and directs the reader's navigation, including a home page with most of the links to the site's content, about, contact, and link page, the URLs of the pages are organized into a hierarchy.

3.1.2 Home Page

The home page of a website is its primary page. The home page is an index or table of contents for other publications stored on the site. There was much progress in metric studies throughout the twentieth century. Librametrics, bibliometrics, scientometrics, informetrics, Webometrics , Cybermetrics, and Altmetrics are metric studies that emerged during the twentieth century. The study of the quantitative aspects of the generation, diffusion, and use of recorded knowledge is known as bibliometrics.

Scientometrics studies quantitative aspects of science as economic activity or discipline. Webometrics is the study of the quantitative part of a web/website.

Infometrics is the study of the quantitative aspect of information.

Cybermetrics is the study of the quantitative aspect of the Internet . Metric studies are a boon to the information science field, which gives information about information and will evolve more in the future.

There is an interrelation between science and scientific communication, which influences information generation. This has been directed towards various phases of scientific communication. Still, it has sought principally to describe the characteristics of the literature available to scientists to identify the required literature or determine how to use it.

A substantial volume of statistical research has expanded my knowledge of scientific literature. The sound effect of this research performance could be realized only through a proper communication system.

It is widely accepted among scientists and social scientists that publishing research in academic and governmental institutions drives high technology and economic growth. Truly, research makes an essential contribution to the economic development of a nation. Such outputs can be used as a yardstick for measuring the quality and quantity of research done in a country or a discipline.

Bibliometrics has been a standard science policy and research management tool in recent decades. All compilations of science indicators significantly rely on publication and citation statistics and more sophisticated bibliometric techniques.

During the last few years, Scientometrics has been increasingly used to evaluate the research performance of scientists and the growth of various disciplines of science. Hence, it implies and induces examination of the nature and extent of contributions made by the scientists of a particular domain or a few significant countries using different primary or secondary sources that facilitate the proper and practical analysis.

3.1.3 Metric Studies

Among the metric studies, bibliometrics first came into existence in 1969. It is a statistical analysis method of publication pattern. Later, all the other metric studies evolved based on the concept of bibliometrics. Metric studies provide enormous, good-quality outcomes in the library and information science field.

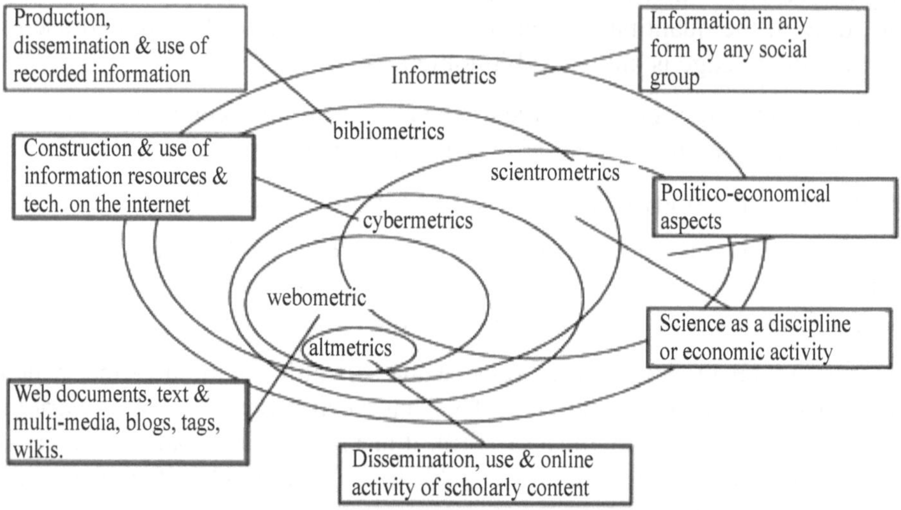

Webometrics uses bibliometric methodologies to study the relationship between different sites on the World Wide Web. Based on the number of times they are hyperlinked to other Websites, such techniques can also be used to map out (called "scientific mapping" in traditional bibliometric research) sections of the Web that appear to be most valuable or influential.

Cybermetrics

Webometrics (Cybermetrics) is a science that attempts to quantify the World Wide Web to learn about the quantity and types of hyperlinks, the structure of the Web, and usage trends. The "Web Impact Factor" (WIF), proposed by Ingwersen, is a reasonably simple metric (1998).

Altmetrics

Altmetrics are non-traditional metrics presented as an alternative to more typical citation impact metrics like the impact factor and h-index in scholarly and scientific publishing. In 2010, the word altmetrics was coined. It is a type of article-level metric originating in the altmetrics hashtag.

When applied to data, metric studies provide additional insights into the data. Metric studies aid in identifying knowledge gaps in specific fields. It promotes new research and generates new thoughts regarding the information. Metric studies benefit the library and information science because they provide information about news. The area of metric studies in library and information science will undoubtedly grow.

3.1.4 Methods of Webometrics

Webometrics research, according to Bjorneborn (2004), includes four main areas:

Web page content and Website link structure analysis (e.g. Hyperlink, Self-link, External link, and Inlink);

Web usage analysis (e.g. exploiting log files for user's searching and browsing behaviour); and

An examination of web technologies (including search engine performance).

As a result, Webometrics is the quantitative study of web-related phenomena, which arose from the realization that bibliometric analytic methods were inadequate.

3.1.4.1 Web Page Content Analysis-

Several Webometrics studies have focused on academic papers rather than websites , using the Internet to track how frequently journal articles are cited. According to Vaughan and Shaw, online citations are generally simple, appearing in journal contents lists rather than reference sections of academic works (Vaughan & Shaw, 2003).

3.1.4.2 Web Link Structure Analysis

Link analysis has been successfully utilized to determine which web pages should be added to the document collection (i.e., which pages to crawl) and sort the documents that fit a user query (i.e., how to rank pages). It has also been used to categorize web pages, find pages connected to provided pages, locate duplicated websites , and solve other information retrieval issues.

3.1.4.3 Web Usage Analysis

The following components cover the web usage analysis -

Web usage pre-processing and novel techniques for discovering and analyzing Web usage patterns.

Log files for the user's searching, browsing behaviour, and log analysis for security applications; and

Web usage pre-processing and novel techniques for discovering and analyzing Web usage patterns.

Web usage mining and analysis that incorporates semantics and domain knowledge.

Webometrics and other related measures are reliable and consistent.

Smart summarization/explanation of changes in Web usage metrics (Thelwall et al., 2005).

3.2 Content Analysis

It is used to see if certain words, themes, or concepts are present in qualitative data (i.e., text). Quantify and examine the presence, meanings, and connections of specific words, themes, or concepts. Researchers can assess the specific terms used in a news story to look for prejudice or partiality. Researchers can deduce the texts' messages, the writer(s), the audience, and even the culture and the period in which the work was produced. Interviews, open-ended inquiries, field study notes, dialogues, or any occurrence of communicative language could be used as data sources (such as books, essays, discussions, newspaper headlines, speeches, media, and historical documents). In a single study, different types of text may be analyzed. The text must be classified or broken down into manageable code categories for analysis (i.e. "codes") before it can be analyzed using content analysis . After the text has been coded into code categories, the codes can be classified into "code categories" to summarise data further.

Three different definitions of content analysis are provided below.

- Definition 1: "Any technique for inferring distinctive properties of messages by systematically and objectively identifying them." (Adapted from Holsti, 1968.)
- Definition 2: "An interpretive and naturalistic approach. It is both observational and narrative and relies less on the experimental elements normally associated with scientific research (reliability, validity, and generalizability) (Ethnography, Observational Research, and Narrative Inquiry, 1994-2012).
- Definition 3: "A study technique for describing the manifest content of communication in an objective, systematic, and quantitative manner."

3.2.1 Uses of Content Analysis-

Determine an individual's, group's, or institution's aims, focus, or communication patterns

Describe how people react to communications regarding their attitudes and behaviours.

Determine a person's or group's psychological or emotional condition

Identify disparities in communication content between countries

Identify communication content patterns

Test and improve an intervention or survey before launching it.

Complement quantitative data with focus group interviews and open-ended queries.

3.2.2 Content Analysis Types

Content analysis can be divided into conceptual analysis and relational analysis. The presence and frequency of concepts in a text are determined by conceptual analysis. The relational analysis builds on conceptual analysis by examining the relationships between concepts in a text. Various outcomes, conclusions, interpretations, and implications can be obtained from each type of analysis.

a. Conceptualization

When most people think of content analysis , they think of conceptual analysis. A concept is chosen for examination in conceptual analysis, and the study comprises quantifying and counting its presence. The primary purpose is to identify the frequency of specific terms appearing in the data. Term definitions might be explicit or oblique. Explicit terms are simple to spot. The coding of implicit phrases is more complex: you must decide on the level of implication and make subjective judgments. As a result, implicit word coding may necessitate the usage of a dictionary, contextual translation rules, or a combination of the two. To start a conceptual content analysis, decide on a research question and a sample or samples to analyze. The text must then be organized into digestible content groups. This is a selective reduction procedure. The researcher can focus on and code for specific terms or patterns that explain the research issue by limiting the text to categories.

3.2.3 Steps to Conduct a Conceptual Content Analysis in General

a) **Choose an analysis level:** word, word sense, phrase, sentence, or theme.

b) **Determine the number of concepts to code for:** Create a list of pre-defined or interactive categories or concepts. Choose between A.

allowing for adding categories during the coding process and B. sticking to the pre-defined set of categories.

Option A includes and analyses new and essential information that may substantially impact the research issue.

Option B allows the researcher to stay focused and look for specific topics in the data.

c) Choose whether to code for a concept's existence or frequency. The coding procedure is altered because of the decision.

When coding for the existence of a concept, the researcher would only count it once if it appeared in the data at least once, regardless of how many times it appeared.

The researcher would count the times a notion appears in a text while coding for its frequency.

d) **Choose how you will distinguish between concepts:** Should text be typed exactly as it appears, or should it be coded the same in all forms? Consider the terms "hazardous" and "dangerousness." The goal is to design coding rules that categorize these word fragments rationally and conspicuously. The guidelines might be written so that all these word segments fall into the same category, or they could be written so that the researcher can separate them into different codes.

e) Create coding rules for your texts. After completing stages 1-4, a researcher can build rules for translating the text into codes. The coding process will be more organized and consistent due to this. The researcher can code for whatever they wish. When the researcher is consistent and coherent in their coding, that is, when they follow their translation guidelines, the validity of the coding process is ensured. Following the translation, guidelines are comparable to validity in content analysis.

f) Determine what to do with irrelevant data: should it be ignored (e.g., common English words like "the" and "and"), or should it be utilized to re-examine the coding scheme if it adds to the coding outcome?

What is the maximum level of the implication that can be used? Is it better to use words that hint at a notion or terms that expressly proclaim it? For instance, "threatening" vs "the individual is frightening" vs "that person might injure me." These words are divided into pieces.

g) **Type the text:** You can do this by hand or software. Researchers can use software to input categories and have the software program code them automatically, rapidly, and efficiently. When coding by hand, a researcher is likelier to notice errors (e.g. typos and misspellings). The text could be cleared of errors and included all accessible info if computer coding is used. This choice between hand and machine coding is especially important for implicit data, where category preparation is critical for accurate coding.

h) **Examine the outcomes:** Wherever possible, draw conclusions and generalizations. Re-examine, ignore, or evaluate the coding system to deal with unnecessary, undesirable, or unused text. Because conceptual content analysis can only quantify information, it is essential to interpret the results carefully. General trends and patterns can be discerned.

3.2.4 Relational Analysis

A notion is examined in relational analysis, like in conceptual analysis. On the other hand, the study comprises investigates the relationships between concepts. Individual conceptions have no inherent value, and meaning is generated from their relationships.

Determine a research question and select a sample before beginning a relational content analysis . The study question must be narrowed so that the concept types can be summarised and are not subject to interpretation. After that, choose some text to analyze. Select text for analysis with care, balancing having enough information for a thorough examination with having a limited amount of information so that findings are not constrained.

Before moving on to the general phases, you can choose from three subcategories of relational analysis.

a. Affect extraction: an emotional assessment of explicit concepts in a text. Emotions vary across time, populations, and places, which is a barrier to this strategy. It may, however, be successful in portraying the speaker's or writer's emotional and psychological state.

b. Proximity analysis: an assessment of the text's explicit concept co-occurrence. Text is a string of words called a "window" scanned for concept co-occurrence.

c. A "concept matrix," or a set of interconnected co-occurring concepts that indicates a more significant meaning, is produced.

d. Cognitive mapping: a graphical tool for extracting effect or analyzing Closeness. Cognitive mapping aims to build a model of the text's overall meaning, such as a graphic map that shows the relationships between concepts.

3.2.4.1 Steps for Conducting a Relational Content Analysis in General

a. Decide on the type of analysis: Once the sample has been chosen, the researcher must decide what types of relationships to investigate and at what level of analysis: word, word sense, phrase, sentence, and themes.

b. Break the text down into categories and code for terms or patterns: A researcher can use coding to check for the presence of meanings or words.

c. Investigate the connections between concepts: Once the words have been coded, the text can be examined for the following:

   Relationship strength: the degree to which two or more concepts are linked.

   Relationship indicator: Are concepts favourably or negatively related?

   Relationship direction: the types of relationships that the categories display. For example, "X implies Y," "X happens before Y", "if X then Y", "if X then Y", "if X then Y", "if X then Y", or "if X then Y."

d. Code the relationships: The statements or relationships between concepts are coded in relational analysis, although in the conceptual analysis, they are not.

e. Conduct statistical analyses: Look for differences or relationships among the identified variables during coding.

f. Lay out representations, such as mental models and decision mapping.

3.2.5 Content Analysis Reliability and Validity

Because of the human character of researchers, coding errors will never be avoided entirely; they can only be reduced. In general, an 80 per cent reliability margin is considered acceptable. Three factors determine a content analysis ' dependability:

a. Stability: the proclivity for programmers to re-code the same material in the same way over time.

b. Reproducibility: the proclivity of a set of coders to classify membership in categories similarly.

c. Accuracy: the degree to which a text's classification statistically correlates to a standard or norm.

Validity

Three criteria determine the content analysis ' validity:

a. Closeness of categories: This can be achieved using multiple classifiers to reach a consensus on each category's definition. A concept category that may be an explicit variable can be expanded to include synonyms or implicit variables using several classifiers.

b. Conclusions: What is the maximum level of the implication that can be used? Do the conclusions correspond to the data? Are there any other factors that could explain the results? This is especially challenging when analyzing and differentiating synonyms with computer software. For example, "mine" might refer to a personal pronoun, an explosive weapon, or a deep hole where ore is retrieved. The frequency and occurrence of that word can be accurately counted using the software.

c. The results' generalizability to a theory is contingent on precise definitions of concept categories, their establishment, and how reliable they measure the notion under consideration. Generalizability is like reliability in that it relies heavily on the three reliability criteria.

3.2.6 Content Analysis' Benefits

- Investigate text-based communication in detail.
- Qualitative and quantitative analyses are both possible.
- Over time, provides vital historical and cultural insights
- Allows for a close relationship with data
- The text can be statistically analyzed in its coded form.
- Provides insight into complicated models of human mind and language use when done correctly
- Is regarded as a relatively "precise" research method when done well
- Content analysis is an easy-to-understand and low-cost research tool.

It becomes a more potent instrument when paired with other research methods, such as interviews, observation, and the utilization of historical records. It is particularly beneficial for analyzing historical material and charting changes across time.

3.2.7 Disadvantages of Content Analysis

Contrary to popular belief, content analysis has several drawbacks.

- It can take a long time to complete.
- Has an enormous risk of error, mainly when the relational analysis is applied to achieve a higher interpretation.
- It frequently lacks a theoretical foundation or attempts to draw relevant generalizations about the linkages and implications revealed in a study far too freely.
- Is inherently reductive, especially when dealing with complex issues.
- Often ignores the context that created the text, as well as the condition of things after the text is produced
- Difficult to automate or computerize etc.

4

Online Ecology

India is considered a pioneer in software development and a favourite destination for IT-enabled services. West Bengal is predominantly an agrarian State. Comprising only 2.7% of India's geographical area, it supports nearly 8% of its population. There are 71.23 lakh farm families, of whom 96% are small and marginal farmers. The average size of land holding is only 0.77 ha. However, the State is bestowed with diverse natural resources and varied agro-climatic conditions that support the cultivation of a wide range of crops.

The net cropped area is 52.05 lakh ha, comprising 68% of the geographical area and 92% of arable land. The cropping intensity is 184%. However, as the State is in the humid tropic and the Bay of Bengal is close by, it often must face natural vagaries like floods, cyclones, hailstorms, etc. Though the State has a surplus production of rice, vegetables and potatoes, a huge gap exists between the requirement and production of pulses, oilseeds, and maize. The deterioration of soil health due to imbalances in chemical fertilizers, the paucity of suitable improved seed varieties, inadequate farm mechanization, unorganized marketing structure, etc., is a major challenge to agricultural growth.

The Agriculture Department works closely with the agro-allied departments, viz. Animal Resources Development, Fisheries, Agricultural Marketing, Horticulture , Cooperation, Water Resources Investigation Development, Irrigation and waterways, Forest, Sericulture , Food and Supplies and WBCADC under the P&RD Department to achieve the above objectives. During recent years, the focus has been on helping small and marginal farmers in their endeavour to get better returns from farming through an improved package of practices, quality inputs, crop diversification, front-ended subsidy for farm mechanization, augmenting irrigation facilities through water conservation and watershed management and by providing market intelligence; the betterment of farmers belonging to SC, ST and backward classes; empowerment of women in agriculture; fostering Public Private Partnership involving the FPOs and NGOs etc. The Department has also launched an ICT -based agri-extension portal, MATIR KATHA (www.matirkatha.gov.in), which provides a dynamic platform to disseminate crop solutions to farmers at the farm-gate level.

West Bengal has comprehensive institutional arrangements of web presence with 19 state-coordinated institutes, 20 ICAR institutions, 12 Private organizations, and 18 NGOs. These numbers still need to be completed as the number of institutions serving agriculture keeps increasing daily. However, there is a clear need to collect more comprehensive and comparable ICT data in India, particularly on the study of websites and their use by individuals, households, and businesses in the agricultural sector. Hence, the current proposed paper attempts to identify and analyze the existing data system of agricultural institution websites in West Bengal.

5

Methods of Inquiry

This chapter deals with an in-depth description of the methods and procedures employed in conducting the research in an organized manner. The research methodology gives the study's work plan. The research objectives and theoretical base offer an initial framework for identifying the appropriate methodology to answer the research questions.

The procedures followed were described under the following headings.

5.1 Research design

5.2 Locale of the study

5.3 Content analysis of websites

5.4 Statistical tools used for the analysis of data.

5.5 Preparation of report

5.1 Research Design

This study aimed to assess the content coverage of agriculture and allied sector websites in West Bengal to determine if they can serve as a one-stop information centre for the stakeholders. The research design adopted for the present study was Content analysis. Content analysis is one of the most suitable methods for systematic analysis and observation to identify detailed information about the unit of analysis.

5.2 Locale of the Study

For any research in social sciences, the situations in which investigations are carried out must give a basic idea to relate the findings to similar problems. The state of West Bengal was purposively chosen for the study as the investigator belonged to the same state. Familiarity with the place of investigation and local language would help the investigator quickly understand the websites available in the local language and facilitate in-depth study.

5.3 Content Analysis of Websites

5.3.1 Selection of Websites

One of the important steps in content analysis is identifying and selecting the study sample or population for the study. Determining the study population in an enormous web corpus is difficult. The very nature of web content selection and analysis raises many methodological issues. There is no standardized formula for selecting the sample for analyzing web content. The momentary nature of web content and continuous updation (instantaneous addition of millions of contents) creates a challenge for web researchers to define the data sample. However, some previous studies have analyzed web content using the following methodologies. Weare and Lin (2000) used the Domain Name System (DNS) for identifying the sampling frame. However, this method was limited as it could not include lower-level links established through top-level domains (TLDs) (McMillan, 2000; Weare& Lin, 2000; Vasantha et al., 2011). McMillan (1997; 1999) and Heo (2007) used search engines to draw sampling frames. However, most documents had yet to be indexed by general search engines such as Google, Yahoo, and others (Bergman, 2001). Weare& Lin, 2000 used collector sites and popular sites or directories for identifying the sampling frame. Even these sites did not provide a complete list of websites , as the lists were incomplete or overlapping.

Since no standard web directory is exclusively dedicated to Indian libraries, the researcher used the Google search engine to identify the sampling frame with an extremely careful examination by eliminating overlapping and duplicate URLs. The population for this study comprised agriculture and allied sector websites in West Bengal . The agriculture and allied sector websites include state-coordinated institutes, ICAR institutions, Private organizations, and NGOs considered for the study. Through the Google web directory, the researcher tried to identify the list of different types of agriculture and allied sector websites, such as state-coordinated institutes, ICAR institutions, Private organizations, and NGOs.

There are 19 state-coordinated institutes, 20 ICAR institutions, 12 Private organizations, and 18 NGOs. Since random sampling does not suit internet-based studies (Bates & Lu, 1997), researchers used non-random or purposive sampling techniques to identify the data sample. After compiling the list of websites , each website's web address or universal resource locators (URLs) were identified through the Google search engine.

The websites containing limited or only a few lines of information were eliminated. Finally, 19 state-coordinated institutes, 20 ICAR institutions, 12

Private organizations, and 18 NGO websites form the data sample for the study (see Appendix B for the list of universities considered for the study).

5.3.2 Unit of Analysis

The unit of analysis is a context from which coding or recording units are drawn for the study (Heo, 2007). The Online Dictionary of Library and Information Science states, "A website is a group of related, interlinked web pages installed on a web server and accessible 24 hours a day to Internet users quipped with browser software. Most websites are created to represent the online presence of a company, organization or institution or are the work of a group or individual" (Reitz, 2010). A website comprises a home page and links for subsequent or secondary-level pages (Vasantha et al., 2011). The present study considered the entire website as a unit of analysis.

5.3.3 Categories in Selection for Data Coding

After selecting the unit of analysis, categories were defined for making valid and replicable inferences from data to their context and for data coding and codebook design (Heo, 2007). As there is no standard method for identifying web-based content features, procedures of previous studies were utilized to construct coding units. The studies considered were:

5.3.4 Variables for Data Coding

The web page contents of the websites have been selected and modified from the scale developed in the studies of Padmannavar & Joshi, 2011 and Bozyigit and Akkankan, 2014. The website content analysis literature used a two-dimensional "available / not available" procedure to assess scale (Bozyigit & Venkan, 2014).

A codebook developed by Wulystan Pius Mtega, 2019 was adopted with suitable modifications for the study to analyze the content information of the websites. The codebook contains the name of the website, title, and keywords;

a form of web content (news articles, Reports, Laws and directives, Statistical data, Training materials, Maps, Contracts, Newsletters, and Speeches); and

The information domain (related to agricultural and allied sectors) and the language of web content.

An inductive analysis technique was used to determine the titles and predominant keywords, which were later used to develop the themes of web content.

The usability of the websites was evaluated by analyzing the thematic areas covered and the aim of the content (teaching/training, research, extension), coverage of the intended audience (internal and external users), and the media presence of the websites.

5.3.5 Code Sheet Development

The web page coding sheet was designed to examine the presence or absence of content related to agricultural and allied sectors. The code book containing mutually exclusive and unambiguous content features was given in the appendix of the thesis.

5.3.6 Coding Procedure and Coder Training

After developing the coding sheet, the researcher was trained to code the content features and the procedure involved in data coding. As recommended by Krippendorf (2004), a pre-test of the data was conducted to establish the reliability of the data with two coders (one, the researcher herself and the chairperson).

5.4 Statistical Tools Used for the Analysis of Data

After data collection, the appropriate statistical technique was used for quantification. The present study used frequency analysis, which summarizes the contents based on the count of incidents found in the sample (Krippendorff, 2004).

5.5 Preparation of Report

The data collected were coded, tabulated, analyzed, and presented in tabular form. The findings were interpreted, and necessary conclusions and inferences were drawn.

6

The Case Study

This chapter deals with the research findings of the study together with a relevant discussion of the facts. Results of the study have been presented, and inferences are drawn from them about the specific objectives of the study set forth. Findings of the present investigation on Webometric Content Analysis of Websites of Agriculture and allied sectors in West Bengal and the inferences drawn from them about objectives are presented under the following headings:

6.1 The current web presence of institutions under agricultural and allied sectors in West Bengal . The number of websites under each sector and their URL domain.

6.2 Contents features of the websites , the form of web contents used, information domain and language used in websites.

6.3 Thematic areas intended audience (internal and external users), and the media presence of the websites .

6.1 Current Web Presence of Institutions Under Agricultural and Allied Sectors in West Bengal

An attempt was made to explore the web presence of the institutions related to agricultural and allied sectors viz-a-viz website domain and URL in West Bengal . The variables like the number of websites , their URL address, and domain use status under different institutions were presented in this section.

6.1.1 Number of Websites under Different Institutions

Table 6.1: Distribution of websites under the various institutional arrangements and URL links.

Sl.No.	Websites	Category	Link
1	Central Institute of Fisheries Education	ICAR Institution	https://cife.edu.in
2	National Dairy Research Institute	ICAR Institution	https://ndri.res.in
3	Central Inland Fisheries Research Institute	ICAR Institution	https://cifri.res.in

Sl.No.	Websites	Category	Link
4	National Institute of Natural Fibre Engineering & Technology	ICAR Institution	www.nirjaft.res.in
5	Central Research Institute For Jute and Allied Fibres	ICAR Institution	https://crijaf.icar.gov.in
6	Central Institute of Freshwater Aquaculture	ICAR Institution	www.cifs.nic.in
7	Bidhan Chandra KrishiViswavidyalaya	ICAR Institution	https://bckv.edu.in
8	Uttar BangaKrishiViswavidyalaya	ICAR Institution	https://ubkv.ac.in
9	Palli Siksha Bhavana	ICAR Institution	https://www.psbvb.in
10	West Bengal University of Animal & Fishery Sciences	ICAR Institution	https://wbuafscl.ac.in
11	Academy of Animal Resources Management	ICAR Institution	https://aarm.ac.in
12	Bengal Veterinary College Research and Development	ICAR Institution	https://www.wbvcrd.in
13	Directorate of Groundnut Research	ICAR Institution	www.dgr.org.in
14	Central Institute of Subtropical Horticulture	ICAR Institution	www.cish.icar.gov.in
15	Indian Veterinary Research Institute, Eastern Regional Station	ICAR Institution	www.ivri.nic.in
16	Central Institute of Fisheries Education, Kolkata	ICAR Institution	www.cife.org.in
17	Central Soil Salinity Research Institute (Regional Research Station)	ICAR Institution	https://cssri.nic.in
18	Indian Council of Agricultural Research	ICAR Institution	https://icar.org.in
19	Central Plantation Crop Research Institute (Regional Station)	ICAR Institution	www.cpcri.icar.gov.in
20	The Directorate of Plant Protection, Quarantine, and Storage	ICAR Institution	http://ppqs.gov.in/regions/cipmcs/rcipmc-kolkata
21	Develop Research Centre and Services Centre	NGO	www.drcsc.org
22	Bharatiya Jana Seva Mission	NGO	https://bjsm.org.in
23	Rural Development Society	NGO	https://www.rudeso.org
24	Kamdebpur Rural Development Society	NGO	http://krdsindia.ngo

Sl.No.	Websites	Category	Link
25	Prasari	NGO	http://www.prasari.org
26	Chakraipur Rural Development Society	NGO	www.chakraipur.org
27	Uttar Dinajpur Agriculture and Farmers Welfare Society	NGO	http://udafws.org.in
28	International Institute of Bengal Basin	NGO	http://iibhb.org.in
29	GobardangaSeba Farmers Society	NGO	https://gsfs.org.in
30	Hazipur Farmers Club	NGO	https://hfc.org.in
31	Krishi Bandha Society	NGO	www.krishibandhansociety.ac.in
32	Farmers Information and Advisory Centre	NGO	https://fiac.org.in
33	Krishnagar Centre For Social Studies and Research	NGO	www.kcssr.org
34	Teesta Jan KrishanKalyan Sangha	NGO	www.tjkksngo.org.in
35	Indian Gramin Services	NGO	www.igsinindia.org.in
36	Tagore Society For Rural Development	NGO	http://tsrd.org.in
37	Parivaar Education Society	NGO	www.parivaar.org.in
38	Aamader Katha	NGO	http://amaderkotha.org.in
39	Lila Agrotech Private Limited	Private Institution	www.lilaagrotech.com
40	PragatiAgri Private Limited	Private Institution	www.pragatiagri.com
41	Nameava Agro Tech Private Limited	Private Institution	https://nameavaago.com
42	Matribhumi Agriculture India Ltd	Private Institution	www.matribhumiagriculturepl.com
43	GuinAgri Solutions Private Limited	Private Institution	www.guinagrisol.com
44	IFFCO	Private Institution	https://iffco.in
45	DhanukaAgritech Private Limited	Private Institution	https://dhanuka.com
46	AnnadhatriAgritech Private Limited	Private Institution	www.annadhatriagritech.co.in
47	Bardhaman Agro Private Limited	Private Institution	https://bardhamanagro.com
48	NabeenKishan Biotechnology Private Limited	Private Institution	https://nabeenkishan.com
49	Janoni Agriculture Private Limited	Private Institution	https://janoniagri.com

Sl.No.	Websites	Category	Link
50	Sashyashree Private Limited	Private Institution	https://sashyashreeagri.in
51	Department of Agriculture and Farmers' Welfare	State Government Websites	http://agricoop.nic.in>west-bengal
52	Wb State Agricultural Marketing Board	State Government Websites	https://wbagrimarketingboard.gov.in
53	Department of Agriculture, West Bengal	State Government Websites	http://matirkatha.gov.in
54	Directorate of Animal Resources and Animal Health	State Government Websites	www.darahwb.org
55	Animal Resources Development, Govt. of West Bengal	State Government Websites	wbard.gov.in
56	Department of Animal Husbandry and Dairying	State Government Websites	https://dahd.nic.in
57	Department of Fisheries, West Bengal	State Government Websites	wbfisheries.in
58	Food and Supplies Department	State Government Websites	https://food.wb.gov.in
59	Department of Food Processing Industries and Horticulture	State Government Websites	https://www.wbfpih.gov.in
60	Department of Forestry , West Bengal	State Government Websites	www.westbengalforest.gov.in
61	Wildlife Conservation	State Government Websites	www.wildbengal.com
62	Wb Forest Dev. Corp. Ltd.	State Government Websites	www.wbfdc.com
63	Irrigation and Waterways Department	State Government Websites	wbiwd.gov.in
64	Department of Micro Small and Medium Enterprise and Textiles	State Government Websites	wbmsmet.gov.in
65	Panchayat and Rural Development	State Government Websites	wbprd.gov.in
66	Self-Help Group and Self Employment	State Government Websites	shgsewb.gov.in
67	Woman and Child Development and Social Welfare	State Government Websites	wbcdwdsw.gov.in
68	Water Resources Investigation and Development	State Government Websites	wbwridd.gov.in
69	Institute of Animal Health and Biologicals, Kolkata	State Government Websites	wbard.gov.in

It was observed from table 6.1 that the institutions were categorized under four sectors: state government institutions, ICAR institutions, Private institutions, and NGOs. Sixty-nine institutions were identified in west Bengal that is working for agricultural and allied sectors. Most of the institutions were under the coordination of ICAR (20), followed by state government (19), NGOs (18), and private institutions (12).

6.1.2 URL Domain

Table 6.2: Distribution of websites based on URL domain.

Sl.No.	URL Domain	State Govt.	ICAR Institutes	Private Institution	NGOs	Frequency (%)
1	.org.in	1	6	0	16	23 (33.33)
2	.gov.in	13	3	0	0	16 (23.18)
3	.com	2	0	9	0	11 (15.94)
4	.in	1	1	3	0	5 (7.24)
5	.nic.in	2	3	0	0	5 (7.24)
6	.ac.in	0	2	0	1	3 (4.34)
7	.res.in	0	3	0	0	3 (4.34)
8	.edu.in	0	2	0	0	2 (2.89)
9	.ngo.in	0	0	0	1	1 (1.44)

Values in the parenthesis () indicate the percentage.

In Table 6.2, in the case of State Government websites , the domain address of 13 websites ended with 'gov.in', 1 with 'org.in', 2 with '.com', 1 with '.in'.

In the case of the ICAR website, six websites ended with 'org.in', three websites ended with 'gov.in', 'nic.in', and 'res.in' Each had ac.in and edu.in domains and 1 with .in domain. Private institutions had the domain addresses of '.com' (9) and '.in' (3). However, NGOs were operating under '.org.in' (16), '.ngo.in' (1), and '.ac.in' (1) URL domains. 7.24% of websites had 'nic.in' and '.in' domains.

The overall status of websites indicated that most of the websites were operating with the domain address 'org.in', (33.33 %), followed by 'gov.in' (23 %), and 'com' (15.9 %). 4.34 % of the website had the domain 'ac.in' and 'res.in' 2.89 % of websites ended with 'edu.in', and only 1.44% had the domain of 'ngo.in'.

All the websites followed character lengths between 3 to 63 and used allowable characters such as letters, digits and hyphens in their domain name (https:// www.registry.in/policies)

6.2 Contents Features of the Websites, the Form of Web Contents, Information Domain and Language used in Websites.

6.2.1 Content features of the websites

Table 6.3: Information regarding the content features of the websites

Sl. No.	Items	State Govt.	ICAR Institutes	Private Institutions	NGOs	Frequency (%)
1	About Us	19	20	12	18	69 (100)
2	Courses/Programs Offered [undergraduate / graduate / postgraduate / distance education/ different trainings]	19	20	12	18	69 (100)
3	Institution contacts information [Email / Phone no / Map of university and collages]	19	20	12	18	69 (100)
4	Recent News	19	20	12	18	69 (100)
5	Faculty contact	19	20	12	18	69 (100)
6	Telephone Directory	19	20	12	18	69 (100)
7	Video / Audio Ideas	19	19	12	18	69 (100)
8	Tenders / Circulars	19	20	12	18	69 (100)
9	Freedom of Information Act / Right to Information Act	19	20	12	18	69 (100)
10	Search Features	17	20	12	18	68 (99)
11	Quick Links	19	19	12	18	68 (98.55)
12	Electronic Media	19	18	12	18	67 (97.1)
13	Publications [University Journals / Books / Publication by Faculty]	19	18	12	18	67 (97.1)
14	Mission	19	17	12	18	66 (95.65)
15	Events	19	20	10	18	66 (96)
16	Forth coming events	19	20	12	14	65 (94)
17	Feedback	16	20	10	16	62 (89.85)
18	Facilities / Amenities and Services	12	20	12	17	61 (88)
19	Placement cell	19	20	10	11	60 (87)
20	Jobs	12	19	11	18	60 (86.95)
21	Departments / Infrastructure	19	16	8	15	58 (84.05)
22	Policy	11	15	11	18	55 (80)
23	Funds	9	16	9	18	52 (75.36)
24	Awards	11	14	8	18	51 (73.91)

Sl. No.	Items	State Govt.	ICAR Institutes	Private Institutions	NGOs	Frequency (%)
25	Admission information / Application [term dates]	12	20	0	18	50 (72.46)
26	Visitors	17	13	9	6	45 (65)
27	Internal social groups / Clubs activities / student union	0	14	12	14	40 (57.97)
28	Faculty research / Case Study	0	17	11	10	38 (55.07)
29	Open Days	6	14	8	7	35 (50.72)
30	Accommodation	0	14	4	11	29 (48.33)
31	Alumni Information	0	11	5	8	24 (34.78)
32	International [support / services]	0	7	8	7	22 (31.88)
33	Accreditation	0	20	5	0	22 (31.88)
34	Health service	0	6	7	5	18 (26.08)
35	Memorandums of understanding with other universities	0	13	2	0	15 (21.74)
36	Scholarship	0	6	0	9	15 (21.74)
37	Library Catalogues	0	12	0	0	12 (17.39)
38	Other information [syllabus, date sheet, revolution forms / procedure]	0	11	0	0	11 (15.94)
39	Scholarship	0	2	0	9	11 (15.94)
40	Students	0	3	0	7	10 (14.49)
41	Culture and Sports	0	5	0	4	9 (13.04)
42	Old Exam papers	0	2	1	0	9 (13.04)
43	Exam Results	0	6	0	0	6 (10.34)

Values in the parenthesis () indicate the percentage

The content features of the websites were analysed and presented in table 6.3.

Results in the table 6.3 revealed that all the websites under the study incorporated content features such as About us,Courses or programs offered, Institutional contact information, Recent news, Faculty contacts, Telephone directory, Video or audio ideas, Tenders/ circulars, right to information act.

99 per cent of the websites contained search features, 98.5 per cent had quick links, and 97.10 per cent of websites had shown media and publications on their web pages.

However, websites lacked much of the content featured on their web pages. Only 15.94 % of the websites contained information about syllabus and scholarship, as only institutional websites information, other websites like government websites or private institutions did not include these data. Only 14.49% of websites informed their students or customers, 13% provided culture and sports information related to old exam papers, and only 10.34 % notified their exam results.

Most of the websites under each sector had provided a generic list of content features that should be available on each website. Based on the domain, the institutions provided relevant information, viz.; the education institution-related websites provided student data such as culture, sports, and examination.

6.2.2 Form of Web Content

Table 6.4: Form of web contents covered by websites -

Sl. No.	Form of Information Resources	State Govt.	ICAR Institutions	Private Websites	NGOs	Frequency (%)
1	Reports	19	20	12	18	69 (100)
2	News Articles	19	18	11	18	66 (95.65)
3	Statistical Data	18	18	12	18	66 (95.65)
4	Speeches	18	17	9	16	60 (86.95)
5	Laws and directives	11	14	12	18	55 (79.71)
6	Contracts	15	17	5	14	51 (73.91)
7	Maps	18	20	5	7	50 (72.46)
8	Training Materials	12	15	6	11	44 (63.76)

Values in the parenthesis () indicate the percentage

It was observed from table 6.4 that all the websites under each sector provided information in the form of reports. 95.65 per cent of the websites used news articles and statistical data forms to provide information. In addition, websites also used speeches (86.95 %), laws and directives (79.71 %), contracts (73.91%), maps (72.46 %) and training materials (63.76 %) for providing information.

It was evident from the table that even though there was a more significant proportion of small and marginal farmers in West Bengal (96.00%) who require information related to different schemes, services, and modern techniques through training mode, there was the most negligible concentration of the institutions for providing information related to training.

6.2.3 Information Domain of the Websites

Table 6.5: Information domain of the websites

Sl.No	Keywords	State Government	ICAR Institutions	Private Institutions	NGOs	Frequency (%)
1	Agriculture	19	12	10	7	48 (69.56)
2	Extension & Rural Livelihood	5	4	1	18	28 (40.58)
3	Horticulture	2	5	8	7	22 (31.88)
4	Forestry	3	3	9	5	20 (28.98)
5	Animal Husbandry	3	8	2	1	14 (20.28)
6	Sericulture	5	3	1	3	12 (17.39)
7	Fishery	1	9	0	1	11 (15.94)
8	Apiculture	4	3	1	3	11 (15.94)

Values in the parenthesis () indicate the percentage.

As per table 6.5, about 70 per cent of the institutions contained information about agriculture. However, less than 50 per cent of the websites provided information such as extension and rural livelihood related (40.58 %), horticulture (31.88 %), forestry (28.98 %), animal husbandry (20.28 %), sericulture (17.39 %), fishery (15.94 %), and apiculture (15.94 %).

So, it was noticed that most websites have keyword 'Agriculture' as West Bengal is economically dependent on agriculture so it would be beneficial and convenient for the farmers.

On the other hand, though West Bengal is the second-largest producer of fish in India and the highest producer of vegetables in India, very few websites informed their users about fishery and apiculture, which shows a lack of awareness among the institutional and governmental officials concerning this matter.

6.2.4 Languages Used in Websites

Table 6.6: languages used in websites

S.no	Languages	State Government	ICAR institutions	Private institutions	NGOs	Frequency (%)
1	English + Bengali	12	3	2	9	26 (37.68)
2	English	5	3	7	9	24 (34.78)
3	English + Hindi	1	14	3	0	18 (26.08)
4	English + Bengali + Hindi	1	0	0	0	1 (1.45)

Values in the parenthesis () indicate the percentage.

It was evident from the table 6.6 that a maximum number of websites (37.68%) used the language both English and Bengali, 34.78% of the websites used only English, 26.08% of the websites used both English and Hindi languages and the least number of websites (1.45%) used all the three languages like English, Bengali, and Hindi.

It can be concluded that there was no website dedicated to only Bengali or only Hindi language. The above table also showed the institutional actors' lack of concern and expertise in providing information through local languages. Each sector should consider providing information in the first language of the state for better communication.

6.3 Thematic Areas, Intended Audience (Internal and External Users), and the Media Presence of the Websites

In this section, the usability of the websites was evaluated by analyzing the thematic areas covered, the information provided by those websites, the coverage of the intended audience (internal and external users), and the media presence of the websites.

6.3.1 Thematic Areas Covered by Web Contents

It could be observed from Table 6.7 that all the web content of websites covered the themes related to agriculture, education, and human rights. Market & MSME (95.65 %) related information was also considered as one of the important themes under the websites.

However, less than one-third of the web contents were related to tribal development & Horticulture & Plantation Crops (31.88%), fisheries (30.40%), forest and wildlife conservation (28.98%) and animal husbandry and dairy (20.3%).

Table 6.7: Thematic Areas Covered by Web Contents

S.no	Information of Websites	State Government websites	ICAR Institutions	Private Institutions	NGO	Frequency (%)
1	Agriculture	19	20	12	18	69 (100)
2	Education	19	20	12	18	69 (100)
3	Human Rights	19	20	012	18	69 (100)
4	Market & MSME	19	20	12	15	66 (95.65)
5	Self-Help Group & Employment	7	20	0	18	45 (65.21)
6	Woman Empowerment	6	20	0	18	44 (63.7)
7	Food Supply & Processing	11	16	8	6	41 (59.42)

S.no	Information of Websites	State Government websites	ICAR Institutions	Private Institutions	NGO	Frequency (%)
8	Health Care of Rural Society	11	14	7	5	37 (53.6)
9	Field Crops &Fibres	5	12	8	10	35 (50.72)
10	Irrigation	11	14	3	5	33 (47.82)
11	Rural Livelihood	5	4	1	18	28 (40.6)
12	Tribal Development	5	11	0	6	22 (31.88)
13	Horticulture & Plantation Crops	2	5	8	7	22 (31.88)
14	Fisheries	5	9	0	7	21 (30.4)
15	Forest & Wildlife Conservation	3	3	9	5	20 (28.98)
16	Animal Husbandry & Dairy	3	8	2	1	14 (20.3)

Values in the parenthesis () indicate the percentage.

Interestingly, even though the state of West Bengal is known for the cultivation practices of horticultural and plantation crops, considerable forest cover, and fisheries, the websites have not shown interest in providing such information.

6.3.2 Coverage of Intended Audience

The findings of Table 6.8 showed that all the websites provided information to audiences like teachers, students, parents, researchers, medium farmers, large farmers, employees, businesspeople, and environmentalists. 88.52% of the websites served the needs of Small and Marginal farmers. 70.49% of the websites fulfilled KVK SMS's demand, followed by women's (50.82).

Table 6.8: Distribution of coverage of intended audience by the websites

S.no	Information of Websites	State Government websites	ICAR Institutions	Private Institutions	NGO	Frequency (%)
1	Teachers	19	20	12	18	69 (100)
2	Students	19	20	12	18	69 (100)
3	Parents	19	20	12	18	69 (100)
4	Researchers	19	20	12	18	69 (100)
5	Medium Farmers	19	20	12	18	69 (100)
6	Large Farmers	19	20	12	18	69 (100)
7	Employees	19	20	12	18	69 (100)
8	Businessmen	19	20	12	15	66 (96.00)
9	Small and Marginal Farmers	9	20	12	18	59 (85.50)

S.no	Information of Websites	State Government websites	ICAR Institutions	Private Institutions	NGO	Frequency (%)
10	KVK SMS	8	20	12	18	58 (84.05)
11	Environmentalist	7	20	12	16	55 (80.00)
12	Land Laborers	11	20	12	11	54 (78.20)
13	Self Help Groups	7	20	0	18	45 (65.20)
14	Joint liability Groups	7	20	0	18	45 (65.20)
15	Women	6	20	0	18	44 (63.70)
16	Artisans	7	17	5	13	40 (57.97)
17	Tribal People	5	11	0	6	22 (31.80)
18	Fishermen	5	9	0	7	21 (30.40)

Values in the parenthesis () indicate the percentage.

However, less than fifty of the websites covered audiences like self-help groups (49.18%), Joint Liability groups (49.18%), Fishermen (47.54%), Land labourers (45.90%), tribal people (44.26%) and artisans (36.06%).

6.3.3 Media Forms of Websites

As per Table 6.9, all the websites (100%) had media elements like text, images, and social media, as everyday users are farmers and working personnel, so these are user-friendly.

60% of the websites showed videos covering their achievements, schemes, and technicalities.

No websites contained animated for their communication purpose.

Table 6.9: Information regarding media forms used by the websites .

S.no	Media forms	State Government	ICAR	Private Institutions	NGO	Frequency (%)
1	Text	19	20	12	18	69 (100)
2	Images	19	20	12	18	69 (100)
3	Social media	19	20	12	18	69 (100)
4	Video	8	13	7	13	41 (59.42)

Values in the parenthesis () indicate the percentage

7

Summary and Conclusion

The quality and effectiveness of extension services are critical to the agricultural sector's long-term viability and output. Farmers have been getting agricultural information from extension workers via interpersonal communication for many years. Still, the number of extension employees has been declining while the number of farming families has increased. As a result, the country's current extension service needs to improve in reaching out to farmers with timely and relevant agricultural information. ICTs are considered a partial answer to quickly getting information to the growing number of farming households because relevant and timely information is vital in agriculture. Farmers may receive up-to-date knowledge and information on agricultural technologies, best practices, markets, price patterns, and customer preferences through its use.

Since farmers in many parts of India, including West Bengal , are becoming more mobile and internet savvy, disseminating useful real-time information about crops, soils, climate, cultivation practices, financing, produce storage, and marketing to farming communities is more important and challenging. Many concerted efforts from the government, non-government organizations, and industry are now required to make our farmers ICT -friendly so that the benefits of rapidly evolving technological advancements in farm production, storage, and marketing can be shared equally among all communities and sectors of farming.

Institutional websites have become one of the most important sources of information for academic and research purposes. Regarding research, educational institutions' websites can proclaim the presence of individuals, research groups, institutions, and departments and publicize their accomplishments. They can also distribute discoveries by publishing summaries, data sets, tools, or hosting web articles. The pages can be made centrally by administrators or web admins or logically by people for their own or research team initiatives. More significant research impact, attracting students, media interest, and business contacts are all potential benefits of having a strong web presence. In this context, it seems sensible to investigate measures of website effectiveness, both to learn more about the communication activity they represent and to develop helpful evaluation metrics. As a result of the privatization of education, it is vital to rate educational institution websites in the context of competition among them. Webometrics is the name given to the method, which entails studying all network-based communications using informetric or other quantitative measures. The use of informetric technologies such as word counts and other comparable techniques to the WWW is evident.

According to a literature review, many studies in foreign nations have been conducted on various aspects of website analysis, such as link structure analysis, which involves the examination of Self Links, Hyperlinks, External Links, Inlinks, and Co-Links. Web Impact Factor, search engine performance, webpage content analysis , and web usage analysis have all been studied.

Given the importance of websites for knowledge management , it is critical to assess how accessible and useful these websites are for the stakeholders to advance farming. In the webometric research in India, only a few studies were found. Considering the above scenario, the following objectives were formulated to analyze the status and approach of institutional web presence.

1. To explore the existence of websites related to Agriculture and allied sectors in West Bengal .
2. To study the webpage content analysis of websites related to agricultural and allied sectors in WB.
3. To analyze the web usage pattern of websites related to agricultural and allied sectors in WB.

This study aimed to assess the content coverage of agriculture and allied sector websites in West Bengal to determine if they can serve as a one-stop information centre for the stakeholders. The research design adopted for the present study was Content analysis. Content analysis is one of the most suitable methods for systematic analysis and observation to identify detailed information about the unit of analysis. After data collection, the appropriate statistical technique was used for quantification, the findings were interpreted, and necessary conclusions and inferences were drawn.

7.1 Summary

Sixty-nine institutions working for agricultural and allied sectors were identified in West Bengal . Most of the institutions were under the coordination of ICAR (20), followed by state government (19), NGOs (18), and private institutions (12).

The overall status of websites indicated that most of them were operating with the domain address' org. in', (33.33 %), followed by 'gov. in' (23 %), and 'com' (15.9 %). 4.34 % of the websites had the domain' ac.in' and 'res.in', 2.89 % of websites ended with 'edu.in', and only 1.44% had the domain 'ngo. in'.

All the websites under the study incorporated content features such as About Us, Courses or programs offered, Institutional contact information, Recent news, Faculty contacts, Telephone directory, Video or audio ideas, Tenders/ Circulars, and the Right to Information Act.

95.65 per cent of the websites used news articles and statistical data forms to provide information. In addition, websites also used speeches (86.95 %), laws and directives (79.71 %), contracts (73.91%), maps (72.46 %) and training materials (63.76 %) for providing information.

About 70 per cent of the institutions contained information about agriculture. However, less than 50 per cent of the websites provided information such as extension and rural livelihood related (40.58 %), horticulture (31.88 %), forestry (28.98 %), animal husbandry (20.28 %), sericulture (17.39 %), fishery (15.94 %), and apiculture (15.94 %).

A maximum number of websites (37.68%) used the language both English and Bengali, 34.78% of the websites used only English, 26.08% of the websites used both English and Hindi languages, and the least number of websites (1.45%) used all three languages like English, Bengali, and Hindi.

All the web content of the websites covered themes related to Agriculture, Education, and Human rights. Market & MSME (95.65 %) related information was also considered as one of the important themes under the websites.

All the websites provide information to audiences like teachers, students, parents, researchers, medium farmers, large farmers, employees, businesspeople, and environmentalists.

All the websites (100%) had media elements like text, images, and social media, as everyday users are farmers and working personnel, so these are user-friendly.

7.2 Conclusion

Considering the real-time information needs of the stakeholders and the vast reach of ICT services in the tech-savvy horizon of the society, all the institutional information providers, such as organizations coordinated under ICAR, state government , NGOs, and private institutions of the West Bengal state, were found present in the website platform. However, there is a need for the creation of guidelines and state-of-the-art facilities to manage information dissemination through websites .

Most websites were found to follow registration process policies, such as using character lengths between 3 and 63 and allowable characters such as letters, digits, and hyphens in their domain name. However, there is a need for scrutiny and close monitoring of the websites before allowing them in the public domain.

Most of the websites under each sector had provided a generic list of content features that should be available on each website. Based on the domain, the institutions provided relevant information, viz., the education institution-related websites provided student data such as culture, sports, and examination.

Even though there was a more significant proportion of small and marginal farmers in West Bengal (96.00%) who require information related to different schemes, services, and modern techniques through training mode, there was the most negligible concentration of the institutions for providing information related to training.

Most websites have the keyword 'Agriculture' as West Bengal is economically dependent on agriculture, so it would be beneficial and convenient for the farmers. On the other hand, though West Bengal is the second-largest producer of fish in India and the highest producer of vegetables in India, very few websites informed their users about fishery and apiculture, which shows a lack of awareness among the institutional and governmental officials concerning this matter.

There was no website dedicated to only Bengali or Hindi language. This showed the institutional actors' lack of concern and expertise in providing information through local languages. Each sector should consider providing information in the state's first language for better communication.

Interestingly, even though the state of West Bengal is known for the cultivation practices of horticultural and plantation crops, considerable forest cover, and fisheries, the websites have yet to show interest in providing such information.

8

Limitations and Future Scope

A student investigator confronted time constraints, such as course credit pressure, and resource constraints, such as physical, budgetary, and managerial constraints, in the current investigation. However, every effort and consideration made the study as objective and scientific as feasible. Despite the researcher's best efforts, the study depends on the respondents' opinions, which may or may not be devoid of their perceptions and biases.

As a result, it is a modest piece of labour that may be completed over a more extended period.

Suggestions for Future Research

- The findings of the present study warrant the need for further investigations in several directions. The following suggestions are made for further research in the following areas.
- The study was confined to one state; therefore, the results cannot be generalised to the whole country. Similar analyses can be taken up in other states to generalise the results.
- The present study has considered only a few selected content features. Several other contents and design features can also be studied.
- A study on the perceptions and behavioural dimensions of the intended audiences towards the websites can be undertaken.
- Similar studies can be repeated regularly to cope with the fast-paced development of information and communications technology.

Bibliography

Acharya, S., & Park, H. W. (2016). Open data in Nepal, a webometric network analysis. Quality & Quantity, 1-17.

Adegbidi, A. B., Mensah, R., Vidogbena, F. and Agossou, D. (2012). Determinants of ICT use by rice farmers in Benin: from the perception of ICT characteristics to the adoption of the technology. Journal of Research in International Business and Management, 2(11): 273-284.

Adigun, T.A. (2002). Analysis of the publications of scientists at the West Africa Rice Development Association, Bouake, Cote d'Ivoire.Quarterly Bulletin of IAALD; 47(2): 43-46.

Agarin, Omoverere and Nwagwu, Williams (2006). Links and Web Impact Analysis of Nigerian Universities, Paper Presented at the International Conference onBridging the Digital Divide in Scholarly Communication in the South, Threats and Opportunities, held at The Netherlands during September 6th to 8th, 2006.

Aguillo, F. Isidro (2009). Measuring the Institution's footprint in the web. Library Hi Tech, 27(4), 540-556.

Aguillo, F. Isidro., et al. (2010). Comparing university rankings. Scientometrics, 85(4),243–256.

Agwu, A. E., Uche-Mba, U. C. and Akinnagbe, O. M. (2008). Use of Information Communication Technologies (ICTs) among Researchers, Extension Workers and Farmers in Abia and Enugu States: Implications for a National Agricultural Extension Policy on ICTs. Journal of Agricultural Extension, 12 (1): 37-49.

Al-shamaileh, Ons , Sutcliffe, Alistair., & Angeli, A.D. (2011). The Effect of Religious Identity on User Judgment of Website Quality. LNCS 6949, p. 620-623.

Albert, C. O. (2014). Constraints to Effective Use of ICT among Extension Professionals & Farmers in Extension Delivery in Rivers State, NIGERIA. Singaporean Journal of business Economics, and Management Studies, 2(11): 136-142.

Alexa Internet (2008). About the Alexa traffic rankings, available at, www.alexa.com (Accessed on 5th August 2016).

Alexa Internet (2008). Alexa history", available at, www.alexa.com. (Accessed on 5th August 2016).

Ali, J. (2011). Factors Affecting the Adoption of Information and Communication Technologies (ICTs) for Farming Decisions. Journal of Agricultural and Food Information: 78-96.

Alimohammadi, Dariush (2006). Webliometrics, a new horizon in information research.Library Review, 55(6),344-348.

All India Survey on Higher Education (AISHE), http://aishe.nic.in/aishe/home (Accessed on 12th March 2017).

Almind, Thomas C., & Ingwersen, Peter. (1997). Informetric Analysis on the World Wide Web, Methodological Approaches to 'Webometrics '. Journal of Documentation, 53(4),404-426.

Aphunu, A. and Atoma, C. N. (2011). Extent of Use of ICTs by Fish Farmers in Isoko Agricultural Zone of Delta State, Nigeria. Journal of Agricultural Extension , 15 (1): 10-21.

Asadi, Maryam and Shekofteh, Maryam (2009). The relationship between the research activity of Iranian medical universities and their web impact factor. The Electronic Library, 27(6),1026 -1043.

Asha, B (2007). Bibliometric properties of 'Demographic India', Annals of Library and Information Studies, June 2007, 54(2),1-11.

Ayoade, A.R. (2010). Effectiveness of Information Sources on Improved Farm Practices among Cowpea Farmers in Oyo State. Global Journal of Human Social Science, 10(4): 39-45.

Bar-Ilan, J. (1997). The "mad cow disease", Usenet newsgroups and Bibliometric laws. Scientometrics, 39 (1), 29-55.

Bar-Ilan, Judit (2008). Methods for measuring search engine performance over time. Journal of the American Society for Information Science and Technology, 53(4), 308-319.

Barjak, Franz, Li, Xuemei & Thelwall, Mike (2006). Which factors explain the web impact of scientists' personal homepages?. Journal of the American Society for Information Science and Technology, 58(2),200-211.

Bates, M. J., & Lu, S. (1997). An exploratory profile of personal home pages: Content, design, metaphors. Online and CD-ROM review.

Berelson, B. (1952).Content Analysis in Communications Research, New York, Free Press.

Berelson, B. and Lazarsfeld, P. F. (1948).The Analysis of Communication Content. Chicago: University of Chicago Press.

Bergman, M. K. (2001). White paper: the deep web: surfacing hidden value. Journal of electronic publishing, 7(1).

Berlo, D.K. (1960).The process of communication: An introduction to theory and practice.New York, Holt, Rinehart and Winston.

Bernad, Harmsen (2000). Adding value to web OPACs. The Electronic Library, 18 (2), 109-113.

Bjorneborn, Lennart (2004). Small-World Linkage and Co-Linkage. Proceedings of the 12th ACM Conference on Hypertext and Hypermedia, New York, ACM Press, p.133-134.

Bjorneborn, Lennart (2004). Small – World link structures across an academic web space, a Library and Information Science approach. Roya[l] School of Library and Information Science, Copenhagen, Denmark, PhD Thesis.

Bjorneborn, Lennart., & Ingwersen, Peter (2001). Perspectives of webometrics .Scientometrics, 50 (1), 65-82.

Bjorneborn, Lennart and Ingwersen, Peter (2004). Toward a basic framework for webomet ric. Journ al of the Ame rican Society for Informati on Science and Technology, 55 (14), 1216-1227.

Bossy, M.J. (1995). The last of the litter, "Netometrics" Available at , http,//biblio- fr.info. unicaen.fr/bnum/jelec/Solaris/d02/2bossy.html (Accessed on 9th November 2016).

Bowler, Leanne, Hong, Wan-Yin., & He, Daqing (2011). The visibility of health web portals for teens, a hyperlink analysis. Online Information Review, 35(3),443-470.

Bozyigit, S., & Akkan, E. (2014). Linking universities to the target market via Web sites: A content analysis of Turkish private universities' Web sites. Procedia-Social and Behavioral Sciences, 148, 486-493.

Buzikashvili, Nikolai (2007). Sliding window technique for web log analysis. Proceedings of the 16th international conference on World Wide Web, held at Banff, Alberta, Canada, 1213-1214.

Catledge, Lara D., & Pitkow, James E. (1995). Browsing Strategies in the World Wide Web. Computer Networks and ISDN Systems, 27(6),1065-1073.

Chakravarty, R., & Wasan, S. (2015). Webometric Analysis of Library Websites of Higher Educational Institutes (HEIs) of India, A Study through Google Search Engine. DESIDOC Journal of Library & Information Technology, 35(5).

Chakravarty, Rupak., & Singh, Sukhwinder (2005). E-Resources for Indian Universities,New Initiatives. SRELS Journal of Information Management, 42(1), 57-73.

Chandrakar, P. (2014). Study on utilization pattern of information and communication technology (ICT) by the agriculture post graduate students, M.Sc. (Ag.) Thesis. Indira gandhi krishi vishwavidyalaya Raipur (C.G.)

Cheng-Zhi, Wang (2005). Evaluating Demographic Websites, Toward Webometric Criteria. Journal of Library and Information Science, 31(2), 52-61.

Damayanti, M. A., Sukmaaji, A., & Suhandiah, S. (2017). Analysis Strategy Visibility And Activity At The Website Stikom. edu In Terms Of Increasing Ranked Webometrics . Jurnal JSIKA, 5(10).

Daudu, S., Chado, S. S. and Igbashal, A.A. (2009). Agricultural Information Sources Utilized By Farmers in Benue State, Nigeria. Production Agriculture And Technology, 5(1): 39-48.

David, Stuart, Thelwall, Mike and Harries, Gareth (2007). UK academic web links and collaboration - an exploratory study. Journal of Information Science, 33 (2),231- 246.

Dawson, K. (1997). "Alexa Internet opens the doors", available at, www.tbtf.com/archive/1997-07-28.html com. (Accessed on 8th August 2016).

Devi, U. and Verma, S. (2011). Farm Women Preference of Communication Sources for Farm Information. Indian Research Journal of Extension Education, 11(2): 15-19.

Didegah, Fereshteh & Erfanmanesh, Mohammad Amin (2010). The study of Malaysian Public Universities' performance on the World Wide Web. Library Hi Tech News, (3),7-11.

Didegah, Fereshteh & Goltaji, Marzieh (2010). Link analysis and impact of top universities of Islamic world on the World Wide Web. Library Hi Tech News, (8),12-16.

Eccles, Kathryn E., & Thelwall, Mike (2012). Measuring the web impact of digitized scholarly resources. Journal of Documentation, 68(4),512-526.

Egghe,L.(2006). Expansion of the field of informetrics, Origins and consequences. Information Processing and Management, 42(6),1405-1407.

Ensminger, D. (1957).A guide to community development. Ministry of Community Development and Cooperation. Govt. of India. New Delhi.

Erfanmanesh, M., & Didegah, F. (2011). Visibility and impact of Iranian research institutions on the web. Library Hi Tech News, 28(1), 4-9.

Fawole, O. Pipy (2008). Pineapple Farmers Information SOURCES and Usage in Nigeria. Bulgarian Journal of Agricultural Science, 14(4): 381-389.

Fischer, R.A., Byerlee, D. and Edmeades, G.O. (2009): Can Technology Deliver On The Yield Challenge To 2050? Expert Meeting on "How to feed the World in 2050", Food and Agriculture Organization of the United Nations and Economic and Social Development Department, Rome.

Flesch, R. (1974). "The art of readable writing". (Rev. Ed.), New York: Harper and Flow.

Fox, J. (1963). "A Comprehension of Coothic Elite and Standard Elite Type Faces."Economics, 6: 93-98.

George, A. L. (1959). "Quantitative and qualitative approaches to content analysis ." In I.D.S. Pool (Eds.), Trends on content analysis. Urbana: University of Illinois Press.

Ghose, Anindya & Yangn, Sha (2008). An empirical analysis of sponsored Searchperformance in search engine advertising. "Proceedings of the international conference on Web search and web data mining 2008", held at Palo Alto, California, USA, February 11-12, 2008, 241-250.

Glover, Eric J. et al. (2002). Using Web Structure for Classifying and Describing Web Pages WWW2002, May 7-11, 2002, Honolulu, Hawaii, USA, ACM 1-58113-449-5/02/0005. Available at,http,//dl.acm.org/citation.cfm?id=511520 (Accessed on 5thOctober 2016).

Gopalakrishnan, S., Ambuja, R., & Seetharama, S. (2002). A Webometric study on library and information science literature. Annals of Library and Information Studies, 49(1),29-35.

Gorai, S. (2015). Perception of farmers towards training programme conducted by Rathindra Krishi Vigyan Kendra: a study in Birbhum district, M. Sc. (Agri.) Thesis, Visva Bharati University

Govindarajan, R., & Dhanavandan, S.,(2016). "Webometric Analysis of Ophthalmology Associations Websites in India", Journal of Advances in Library and Information Science, 5(4), 359-366.

HENDRIKX, B., DORMANS, S., LAGENDIJK, A., & Thelwall, M. (2017).Understanding the geographical development of social movements, a web□link analysis of Slow Food. Global Networks, 17(1), 47-67.

Heo, S. (2007). The potential of the Internet in arts management: content analysis of arts organization websites (Doctoral dissertation, RMIT University).

Hirata, Yoko & Hirata, Yoshihiro (2009). Students' Evaluation of Websites in Hybrid Language Learning. F.L. Wang et al. (Eds.). ICHL 2009, LNCS 5685, p.186-196.

Holmberg, Kim (2010). Co-inlinking to a municipal Web space, a webometric and content analysis . Scientometrics, 83(4), 851-862.

http, //en.wikipedia.org/wiki/Internet (Accessed on 12th August 2016).

http, //www.findmehere.com/search/dictionary/w/webpage .htm (Accessed on 12th August 2016).

http, //www.inflibnet.ac.in/infonet/introduction.php (Accessed on 12th October 2016).

Hudeckova , H. and Lostak, M. (2004). "SAPARD: experiences and challenges for the sure". Zemedelska Ekonomika; 50(4): 152-160.

Huntington, Paul (2006). Obtaining subject data from log files using deep log analysis,case study OhioLINK. Journal of Information Science, 32(4), 299-308.

Huntington, Paul, Nicholas, David & Jamali, Hamid R. (2008). Website usage metrics, A re-assessment of session data. Information Processing and Management, 44(1),358-372.

Ingwersen, Peter (1998). The calculation of web impact factors". Journal of Documentation, 54 (2), 236-243.

Ingwersen, Peter (2006). Webometrics , ten years of expansion. In "Proceedings International Workshop on Webometrics, Informetrics and Scientometrics & Seventh COLLNET Meeting", held at Nancy (France). May 10-12, 2006.

Iroaganachi, M. A., Ilogho, J. E., Itsekor, V. O., & Osinulu, I. (2016). Research Output and Sustainable Development, Webometric Analysis of Scopus Indexed Publications 2008-2014.

Isfandyari-Moghaddam, A., Danesh, F., & Hadji-Azizi, N. (2015). Webometrics as a method for identifying the most accredited free electronic journals, The case of medical sciences. The Electronic Library, 33(1), 75-87.

Islam, M.A., & Alam, M.S. (2011). Webometric study of private universities in Bangladesh. Malaysian Journal of Library & Information Science, 16(2), 115□126.

Islam, Md. Anwarul. (2011). Webometrics study of Universities in Bangladesh. Annals of Library and Information Studies, 58(3), 307-318.

Jalal, S.K., Biswas, S.C., & Mukhopadhyay, P. (2009). Bibliometrics to Webometrics .Information Studies, 15(1), 3-20.

Jalal, S.K., Biswas, S.C., & Mukhopadhyay, P. (2010). Web Impact factor and link analysis of selected Indian universities. Annals of Library and Information Studies, 57 (2), 109-121.

Jalal, S.K., Biswas, S.C., & Mukhopadhyay, P. (2010). Web Presence of Selected Asian Countries, A Webometric Study. Collnet Journal of Scientometrics and Information Management, 4(2), 1-12.

Janis , I.L. (1965). "The problem of validating content analysis ". In Harold D. Lasseweell, Nathan Leites and Associates(Eds). Language of politics: Studies in quantitative semantics (pp.55-82). Cambridge: MIT Press. (Original work published

Jeyshankar, R. & Ramesh Babu, B. (2009). Websites of universities in Tamil Nadu, a webometric study. Annals of Library and Information Studies, 56(2), 69-79.

Jeyshankar, R., Ramesh Babu, B., & Nageswara Rao, P. (2009). Measuring the Web Impact Factor of State Agricultural Universities Websites in India. Indian Journal of Agricultural Library and Information Services, 25 (1), 1-14.

Jeyshankar, R. Ramesh Babu, B & Gopalakrishnan, S. (2009). Basic frame work of webometric study, A study. KELPRO Bulletin, 13(1), 4 1-48.

Jose, Luis Ortega, Isidro, F. Aguillo & Joss, Antonio Prieto (2006). Longitudinal Study of Contents and Elements in the Scientific Web environment. Journal of Information Science, 32(4),344-351.

Jowkar, Abdolrasoul & Didegah, Fereshteh (2010). Evaluating Iranian newspapers' web sites using correspondence analysis. Library Hi Tech, 28(1),119-130.

Jung, K., & Park, H. W. (2016). Tracing inter organizational information networks during emergency response period, A webometric approach to the 2012 Gumi chemical spill in South Korea. Government Information Quarterly, 33(1), 133-141.

Kabir, K. H. (2015). Attitude and Level of Knowledge of Farmers on ICT based Farming. European academic research, Vol. II: 13177-13196.

Kanellopoulos, Dimitris & Kotsiantis, Sotiris (2012). Evaluating and recommending Greek newspapers' websites using clustering. Program, electronic library and information systems, 46(1),71-91.

Kastania, A.N. & Zimeras, Stelios (2010). Evaluation for Web-Based Applications.Annals of Information Systems 7, Springer Science+Business Media, LLC 2010.

Kayal, B.S. (1975). "A study of sources of information, readership and content in Sengali farm magazine "Krishi Pragati' in West Bengal ". Unpublished M.Sc. thesis. Division of Agricultural Extension . IARI, New Delhi.5

Kelsey, L.D. and Hearne, C.C. (1965). "Co-operative Extension Work", New York Comstock Publishing Associates.

Kent, Allen. (1997). Encyclopedia of Library and Information Science. New York, Marcel Dekkar. 19.

Kim, Yong Mi (2011). Users' perceptions of university library websites , A unifying view. Library & Information Science Research, 33(1), 63-72.

Kousha, K. (2003). A comparison of Iranian newspaper websites with the application ofweb impact factor (WIF), Ettela'Shenasi, 287-114.

Krippendorff, K. (2004). Reliability in content analysis : Some common misconceptions and recommendations. Human communication research, 30(3), 411-433.

Kumar, K. (2017). Web Impact Factor Analysis for Deemed Universities in Andhra Pradesh. DESIDOC Journal of Library & Information Technology, 37(2).

Kumar, K. (2017). Web Impact Factor Analysis for Deemed Universities in Andhra Pradesh. DESIDOC Journal of Library & Information Technology, 37(2).

Lal, C., & Kumar, K (2007). Descriptive questions in Library and Information science.Ess Ess Publication, New Delhi.

Lang,P., Gouveia, F.C., & Leta, J. (2010). Site co-link analysis applied to small networks, a new methodological approach. Scientometrics, 83(1), 157-166.

Larson, Ray R. (1996). Bibliometrics of the World Wide Web, An Exploratory Analysis of the Intellectual Structure of Cyberspace, In Proceedings American Society for Information Science, Available at,https,//sherlock.ischool.berkeley.edu/asis96/asis96.html (Accessed on 6th March 2017).

Lee, Moosung & Park, H.W. (2012). Exploring the web visibility of world-class universities. Scientometrics, 90(4),201-218.

Lee J, H., & Hong, G, H. (2005). Incorporating Web Intelligence into Website Evolution. 3611, 710-713.

Li, Xuemei (2003). A review of development and application of the web impact factor.Online Information Review, 24 (6), 407- 417.

Liu, Yigun et al. (2007). Automatic search engine performance evaluation with click- through data analysis. Proceedings of the 16th international conference on q World Wide Web 2007, Banff, Alberta, Canada May 08 - 12, 2007, 1133-1134.

Lokeswari, K. (2016). A Study of The Use Of ICT Among Rural Farmers. International Journal of Communication Research: 232-238.

Madhuri, A. J., Surendra Babu, K. & Ramesh, A. (2013). Webometric Analysis of State Universities in Andhra Pradesh, A study. International Journal of Library and Information Studies, 3 (1), 65-78.

Madhusudhan, M. & Prakash, S. (2013). Websites of Indian Institutes of Technology, A Webometric Study. International Journal of Library and Information Studies, 3(4), 93-107.

Maharana, R.K., Panda, K.C., & Sahoo, J. (2012). Web Impact Factor (WIF) and Link Analysis of Indian Institute of Technologies (IITs), A Webometric Study. Library Philosophy and Practice, Paper 789.

Malgeri, Michele. Longheu, Alessandro & Carchiolo, Vincenza (2005). Information categorization in web pages and sites. Web Intelligence and Agent System, 3(3), 183-198.

Maltseva, A. A., Veselov, I. N., & Barsukova, N. E. (2015). Research on image capital of state scientific centers in Russian Federation using the webometrics tools. Aktual'ni Problemy Ekonomiky= Actual Problems in Economics, (173),444.

Markov, A.A. (1913). Essai d'une recherché statisque sur le texte du roman "Euge Onegin" illustrant la liaison des epreuves en chaine (Russian). Bulletin de l'Acaderimperiale des Sciences de St. Petersbourg.6(7): 153-162.

Martín-Martín, A., Orduña-Malea, E., Ayllon, J. M., & López-Cózar, E. D. (2016). The counting house, measuring those who count. Presence of Bibliometrics, Scientometrics, Informetrics, Webometrics and Altmetrics in the Google Scholar Citations, ResearcherID, ResearchGate, Mendeley & Twitter. arXiv preprint arXiv,1602.02412.

Mathur, I.N., Singh, K.N. and Das, K.K. (1978). "Readership training, nature of content and sources of information of farm periodicals in India". Indian Journal of Extension Education, 14: 3 & 4, pp.39-44.

Mayr, Philipp & Walter, Anne-Kathrin (2007). An exploratory Study of Google Scholar.Online Information Review, 31(6),814-830.

Mburu, P. (2013). Factor Influencing Access to Agricultural Information by Smallholder Farmers Through ICT Channels In Deiya Location Kiambu County, M. Sc. (Agri.) Thesis, University of Nairobi.

McMillan, J. H. (2000). Fundamental assessment principles for teachers and school administrators. Practical Assessment, Research, and Evaluation, 7(1), 8.

McMillan, R. (1999). Competition, parental involvement, and public school performance. Stanford University.

McMillan, R. (2000, January). COMPETITION, PARENTAL INVOLVEMENT AND PUBLIC-SCHOOL PERFORMANCE. In Proceedings. Annual Conference on Taxation and Minutes of the Annual Meeting of the National Tax Association (Vol. 93, pp. 150-155). National Tax Association.

McMillan, S. J. (1999). Health communication and the Internet : Relations between interactive characteristics of the medium and site creators, content, and purpose. Health Communication, 11(4), 375-390.

Miah, A. M., Sarker, A., Dev, D. S., and Kabita, K. N. (2016). Preference of information sources by the fish farming communities of Muktagacha Upazila in Bangladesh. Journal of Agricultural Extension and Rural Development, 8(9): 160-170.

Mittal, S. & Mittal, M. (2015). Socio-economic Factors Affecting Adoption of Modern Information and Communication Technology by Farmers in India: Analysis Using Multivariate Probit Model. The Journal of Agricultural Education and Extension : 1-14.

Mittal, S. and Mehar, M (2012). How Mobile Phones Contribute to Growth of Small Farmers? Evidence from India. Journal of International Agriculture: 227-244.

Moses, Boudourides, Beatrice, Sigrist & Philippos, Alevizos D. (1999). Webometrics and the Self-Organization of the European Information Society, Webometrics and the SOEIS, Draft Report Task 2.1 of the Soeis Project Rome Meeting June 17-19, 1999. Available at, http..//hyperion.math.upatras.gr/webometrics /(1de22) [29/10/200318,50,12] (Accessed on 5th January 2017).

Mtega, W. P. (2019). Content coverage in local government authority websites in Tanzania: a web content analysis . University of Dar es Salaam Library Journal, 14(1), 82-97.

Mukherjee, Bhaskar (2009). Link Analysis of Indian political parties' web sites, a temporal comparison. Annals of Library and Information Studies, 56 (3), 201-211.

Mukherjee, Bhaskar (2009). Link Analysis of Indian political parties' web sites, a temporal comparison. Annals of Library and Information Studies, 56 (3),201-211.

Mukhopadhyay, Parthasarathi (2004). Measuring Web Impact Factors, A Webometric Study based on the Analysis of Hyperlinks, Proceedings of National Seminar on Information Support for Rural Development, December 2005, IASLIC, Available at, http, //drtc. isibang.ac.in/oai/request (Accessed on 17th March 2017).

Mukhopadhyay, Parthasarathi (2005). Measuring Web Impact Factors, A Webometric Study based on the Analysis of Hyperlinks, Proceedings of National Seminar on Information Support for Rural Development, December 2005, IASLIC, Available at, http,//drtc. isibang.ac.in/oai/request. (Accessed on 5th October 2016).

Murthy.T.A.V., Cholin,V.S., & Vijayakumar, J.K. (2005). UGC-INFLIBNET Initiatives In, E-Journal Consortia and Digital Library of Doctoral Theses for Indian Universities. Proceedings of National Conference on Digital Library and e-Theses (NCDLET 2005) held on January 7-8, 2005 at Jadavpur University, Kolkata.

Namenwrith, J.Z. and Weber, R.P. (1987) "Dynamics of culture." Winchester, MA Alllen and Unwin.

Nesset, Valerie (2011). Following the Signs, Children's Use of Visual Cues to Facilitate Website Evaluation. LNCS 6764, p.599-606.

Nicholas, David, Huntington, Paul & Homewood, Janet (2003). Assessing used content across five digital health information services using transaction log files. Journal of Information Science, 29(6),499-515.

Nicholas, David et al. (1999). Cracking the code, web log analysis. Online Information Review, 23(5),263-269.

Nicholas, David et al. (2000). Evaluating consumer website logs, a case study of the Times/The Sunday Times website. Journal ofInformation Science, 26(6),399-411.

Ninkov, A., & Vaughan, L. (2017). A webometric analysis of the online vaccination debate. Journal of the Association for Information Science and Technology.

Noruzi, A. (2006). The web impact factor, a critical review. The Electronic Library, 24(4), 490-500.

Noruzi, Alireza (2005). Web Impact Factors for Iranian Universities, Webology. Volume 2, Number 1, Available at, http,//www.webology .ir/2005/v2n1/a11.html. (Accessed on 5th October 2016).

OECD (2002) Frascati Manual, proposed standard practice for surveys on research and experimental development, 6th edition. Retrieved 27 April 2017 from www.oecd.org/sti/frascatimanual.

Opara, U. N. (2008). Agricultural Information Sources Used by Farmers in Imo State, Nigeria. SAGE journal, 24(4): 289-295.

Ortega, Jose Luis & Aguillo, Isidro F. (2007). Visualization of the Nordic academic web, Link analysis using social network tools. Information Processing and Management, 44(4),1624-1633.

Ortega, José Luis & Aguillo F. Isidro (2011). Social Network Tools for the Assessment of the University Web Performance. Social Media Tools and Platforms in Learning Environments, Springer-Verlag Berlin Heidelberg.

Osareh, F. (2003). Mapping the structure of library and information schools (LIS) websites using cluster and multi-dimensional", paper presented at the 9th International Conference on Scientometrics and Informetrics, Beijing, 25-29 August.

Osondu, C. K. and Ibezim, G. M. C. (2015). Awareness and Perception of Farmers to the Use of Information and Communication Technologies (ICTs) in Agricultural Extension Service Delivery: A Case Study of Imo State, Nigeria. International Journal of Agriculture Innovations and Research, 4(1): 55-60.

Owen, Thomas (2000). Webometric analysis of departments of librarianship and Information Science. Journal of Information Science, 26 (6), 421-428.

Padmannavar, S., & Joshi, M. J. (2011). A survey analysis of National and International University Websites contents. International Journal of Computer Applications, 33(6), 49-58.

Paisely W. (1990). The future ofbiblimetrics. In, Borgman Christine L. Scholarly Communication and Bibliometrics. Sage, London, 281-299.

Pandey, R. and Mehta, S. (2002). Awareness of Educational Technologies in Open Learning System by Target Group. Indian Journal of Social Research, 43(3): 183-189.

Pandey, R. and Mehta, S. (2003). Extent of Use of Educational Technologies by Distance Learners-A Study. Indian Journal of Social Research, 44(4): 341-345.

Papachristos, Eleftherios and Avouris, Nikolaos (2011). The Application of Preference Mapping in Aesthetic Website Evaluation. LNCS 6949, 616–619.

Park, Han Woo & Thelwall, Mike. (2003). Hyperlink Analysis of the World Wide Web, A Review. Journal of Computer Mediated Communication, 8(4). Available at, http.//www.ascusc.org/jcmc/vol8/ issue4/park. html. (Accessed on 5th January 2017).

Park, Han Woo (2004). Presence of Taiwan on the World Wide Web in South Korea, dynamics of digital and geographical presence on cyberspace. The International Information & Library Review, 36(4),329-340.

Park, Soyeon, Lee, Joon Ho & Bae, Hee Jin (2005). End user searching, A Web log analysis of NAVER, a Korean Web search engine. Library and Information Science Research, 27(2),203-221.

Payne, Nigel & Thelwall, Mike (2004). A Statistical Analysis of UK Academic Web Links. Cybermetrics, 1 (2). Available athttp, //cybermetrics.cindoc.csic.es/articles/v8i1p2.html. (Accessed on 3th January 2017).

Payne, Nigel & Thelwall, Mike (2005). Mathematical models for academic webs, Linear relationship or non-linear power law? Information Processing & Management, 41(6),1495-1510.

Payne, Nigel & Thelwall, Mike (2008). Do academic link types change over time?Journal of Documentation, 64(5),707-720.

Payne, Nigel & Thelwall, Mike (2008). Longitudinal trends in academic web links.Journal of Information Science, 34(1),3-14.

Pechnikov, A. A., & Nwohiri, A. M. (2012). Webometric analysis of Nigerian university websites . Webology, 9(1), Article 96. Available at, http,//www.webology.org/2012/v9n1/a95.html. (Accessed on 5th December 2016).

Pinto, María et al. (2007). Metric analysis of the information visibility and diffusion about the European Higher Education Area on Spanish University websites . Scientometrics, 72(2),345-370.

Power, K.B., Expanding Domains in Indian Higher Education. New Delhi, Association of Indian Universities, 2012.

Promila and Sushma Kaushik, (2000), Content analysis of Home Science Extension Research, IJEE, Vol. XXXVI No. 3 & 4.

Raghuprasad, K. P., Devaraja, S.C and Gopala, Y. M (2013). An analysis of knowledge level of farmers on utilisation of ict tools for farm communication. Journal of Rural Development, Vol. 32: 301-310.

Ramesh Babu, B & O'Brien, Ann (2000). Web OPAC interfaces, an overview". The Electronic Library, 18(5), 316-327.

Ramesh Babu, B., Jeyshankar, R. & Nageswara Rao, P. (2009). Measuring the Web Impact Factor of State Agricultural Universities Websites in India. Indian Journal of Agricultural Library and Information Services, 25(1),1-14.

Ramesh Babu, R., Jeyshankar & Rao P. N. (2010). Websites of Central Universities in India, A Webometric Analysis. DESIDOC Journal of Library & Information Technology, 30(4),33-43.

Ranganatham, S.R. (1969). Library and its scope. Bangalore, DRTC Seventh Seminar Volume, paper DA, 1995, 285-301. International Journal of Scientometrics and Informetrics, 1 (1), 15-21.

Ranking World Universities Websites http, //www.webometrics .info/en (Accessed in 12th February 2017).

Rees, D., Momanyi, M., Wekundah, J., Ndungu, F., Odondi, J., Oyure, A. O., Andima, D., Kamau, M., Ndubi, J., Musembi, F., Mwaura L. and Joldersma, R. (2000). Agricultural knowledge and information systems in kenya – implications for technology dissemination and development. Agricultural Research & Extension Network.

Rehman, F., Muhammad, S., Ashraf, I., Mahnood, Ch., Ruby, T. and Bibi, I. (2013). Effect of farmers' socioeconomic characteristics on access to agricultural information: Empirical evidence from Pakistan. The Journal of Animal & Plant Science, 23(1): 324-329.

Riddler, N. and Hashamunda, N. (2001). Promotion of sustainable commercial aquaculture in sub-Sahara Africa. Vol.1. Policy Framework. F.A.O Fisheries Technical Paper, No. 408/1/ Rome, F. A.O. 15-17, 32-33.

Romero-Frías, Esteban & Vaughan, Liwen (2010). Patterns of web linking to heterogeneous groups of Companies. The case of stock exchange indexes. Aslib Proceedings, New Information Perspectives, 62(2),144-164.

Rousseau, Ronald (1997). Citations, an exploratory study. Cybermetrics, 1(1), 1. Available at, http,//www.cindoc.csic.es/ cybermetrics/ articles/v1i1p1.html (Accessed on 5th October 2016).

Sabyasachi Roy, N. S. Verma, S. N. Laharia and Anjali Sarangi, (2005), Content and Coverage of Farm News of leading Bengali Dailies, Vol. 41, No. 1 & 2.

Sadat-Moosavi, Ali & Tajeddini, Oranus (2012). Accessibility of online resources cited in scholarly LIS journals A study of Emerald ISI-ranked journals. Aslib Proceedings, New Information Perspective, 64 (2),178-192.

Samir, Kumar Jalal, Subal, Chandra Biswas & Mukhopadhyay, Parthasarathi. (2009). Bibliometrics to Webometrics . Information Studies, 15 (1), 40-49.

Sebeok, T. A. and Zeps, V.J. (1958). "An analysis of structured content with application of electronic computer research in psycholinguistics". Language and Speech, 1: 181-193.

Sengupta, I. N. (2009). Bibliometrics, Informetrics, Scientometrics and Librametrics, An Overview. International Journal of Libraries and Information Services. 42(2), 75– 98.

Sharma, M., kaur, G., and Gill, M. S. (2014). Use of Information and Communication Technology in Agriculture by Farmers of District Kapurthala. Journal of Krishi Vigyan: 83-89.

Shukla, Akhandanand & Tripathi, Aditya (2009). Webometric Analysis of Institutes of National Importance in India. IASLIC Bulletin, 54 (3),165-180.

Shukla, S.H., & Poluru, L. (2012). Webometric Analysis and Indicators of Selected Indian State Universities. Information Studies, 18(2), 79-104.

Sireesha, P., Rao, B. S. and Raju, D.T. (2014). Constraints Encountered in the Utilization of Information and Communication Technology (ICT) Tools by Various Animal Husbandry (A.H.) Organizations in Andhra Pradesh. International Journal of Innovative Research in Science, Engineering and Technology, 3(6): 13693-13701.

Smith, A. (2005). Citations and links as a measure of effectiveness of online LISjournals. IFLA Journal, Official Journal of the International Federation of Library Associations and Institutions ,31(1),75-84.

Smith, Alastair G. & Thelwall, Mike (2002). Web Impact Factors for Australasian universities. Scientometrics, 54(3),363-380.

Smith, Alastair G. (1999). ANZAC Webometrics , exploring Australasian Web structures Available at, http,//www.csu.edu.au/special/online99/ proceedings99/203b.htm1de13) [27/10/200818,14,40] (Accessed on 21th December 2016).

Smith, Alastair G. (1999). A Tale of Two Web Spaces, Comparing Sites Using Web Impact Factors. Journal of Documentation, 55(5),577-592.

State Universities in South India http,//www.ugc.ac.in/stateuniversity.aspx (Accessed on 15th August 2016).

Sugak D.B. (2011). Rankings of a University's Web Sites on the Internet . Scientific and Technical Information Processing, 38(1),17-19.

Sujitha, Maria & Jeyshankar, R (2013). Web Page Analysis of Indian Institute of Technologies' (IITs) Websites, A webometric Study, International Journal of Digital Library services, 3(1),55-65.

Sujitha, Maria & Jeyshankar, R. (2012). Link Structure and Web Impact Factor of ICMR Institutes in India, A Study. SALIS Journal of Library and Information Science, 4(1-4),10-20.

Svetal, Shukla & Lalitha, Poluru (2012). Webometric Analysis and indicators of selected Indian state universities. Informetrics, 18 (2),79-104.

Syiem, R. and Raj, S. (2015). Access and Usage of ICTs for Agriculture and Rural Development by the tribal farmers in Meghalaya State of North-East India. Journal of Agricultural Informatics: 24-41.

Tague-Sutcliffe, J. (1992). An Introduction to informetrics. Information Processing and Management, 28 (1), 1-3.

Thanuskodi, S. (2011). Webometric Analysis of Private Engineering College Websitesin Tamil Nadu. Journal of Communication, 2(2), 73-81.

Thelwall, M. (2008). Quantitative Comparisons of Search Engine Results. Journal of the American Society for Information Science and Technology, 59 (11), 1702-1710.

Thelwall, M. (2011). A comparison of link and URL citation counting. Aslib Proceedings, New Information Perspectives, 63(4), 419-425.

Thelwall, M., Kousha, K., Dinsmore, A., & Dolby, K. (2016). Alternative metric indicators for funding scheme evaluations. Aslib Journal of Information Management, 68(1), 2-18.

Thelwall, Mike & Harries, Gareth (2004). Do The Websites of Higher Rated Scholars Have Significantly More Online Impact? Journal of the American Society for Information Science and Technology, 55(2),149-159.

Thelwall, Mike & Harries, Gareth (2004). Web Pages that Link to Universities Yield Information about the Wider Dissemination of Research? Journal of Information Science, 30(3),240-253.

Thelwall, Mike & Vaughan, Liwen (2004). Webometrics , An Introduction to the special issue. Journal of the American Society for Information Science and Technology, 55(14),213-1215.

Thelwall, Mike & Wilkinson, David (2002). Graph Structure in Three National Academic Webs, Power Laws with Anomalies. Journal of the American Society for Information Science and Technology, 54(8),706-712.

Thelwall, Mike & Wilkinson, David (2003). Three Target Document Range Metrics for University Websites. Journal of the American Society for Information Science and Technology, 54(6),489-496.

Thelwall, Mike (2000). Web Impact Factors and Search Engine Coverage. Journal of Documentation, 56(2),185-189.

Thelwall, Mike (2001). Extracting Macroscopic Information from Web Links. Journal of the American Society for Information Science and Technology, 52(13),1157- 1168.

Thelwall, Mike (2001). Results from a Web Impact Factor crawler. Journal of Documentation, 57 (2),177-191.

Thelwall, Mike (2001). Web log file analysis, backlinks, and queries. ASLIB Proceedings, 53(6),217-223.

Thelwall, Mike (2002). An Initial Exploration of the Link Relationship bet ween UK University Websites. ASLIB Proceedings, 54(2),118-126.

Thelwall, Mike (2002). A Research and Institutional Size Based Model for National University Website Interlinking. Journal of Documentation, 58(6), 683-694.

Thelwall, Mike (2002). Conceptualizing documentation on the web, an evaluation of different heuristic – based models for counting links between university websites . Journal of the American Society for Information Science and Technology, 53(12),995-1005.

Thelwall, Mike (2002). Evidence for the existence of geographic trends in university website interlinking. Journal of Documentation, 58 (5), 563-574.

Thelwall, Mike (2002). Methodologies for crawler-based Web surveys. Internet Research, Electronic Networking Applications and Policy, 12(2),124-138.

Thelwall, Mike (2003). Web use and peer interconnectivity metrics for academic websites . Journal of Information Science, 29(1),1-10.

Thelwall, Mike (2003). What is this link doing here? Beginning a fine-grained process of identifying reasons for academic hyperlink creation. Information Researc h an International Electronic Journal, 8 (3). Available at, http,//informationr.net/ir/8- 3/ paper151.html (Accessed on 25th July 2016).

Thelwall, Mike (2004). Interpreting Social Science Link Analysis Research, A Theoretical Framework. Journal of the American Society for Information Science and Technology, 57 (1),60-68.

Thelwall, Mike (2008). Bibliometrics to Webometrics . Journal of Information Science,34(4),605-621.

Thelwall, Mike (2008). Quantitative Comparisons of Search Engine Results. Journal of the American Society for Information Science and Technology, 59(11), 1702-1710.

Thelwall, Mike (2009). Introduction to Webometrics , Quantitative Web Research for the Social Sciences. Morgan & Claypool. http, //www.morganclaypool.com/ doi/abs/.com (Accessed on 5th August 2012).

Thelwall, Mike (2011). A Comparison of link and URL citation counting. Aslib Proceedings, New Information Perspectives, 63(4),419-425.

Thelwall, Mike (2006). Commercial Website links. Internet Research, Electronic Networking Applications and Policy, 11(2),114-124.

Thelwall, Mike., Vaughan, Liwen and Björneborn, Lennart (2005). "Webometrics ".Annual Review of Information Science and Technology, 39, 81-135.

Thelwall, Mike and Harries, Gareth (2002). The Connection between the Research of a University and Counts of Links to its Web Pages, An Investigation Based Upon a Classification of the Relationships of Pages to the Research of the Host University. Journal of the American Society for Information Science and Technology, 54(7),594-602.

Thelwall, Mike et al. (2001). Custom interfaces for advanced queries in search engines.ASLIB Proceedings new information perspectives 2001, 53 (10),413-422.

Thelwall, Mike et al. (2002). European Union associated university websites . Scientometrics, 53(1),95-111.

Vasantha Raju, N., & Harinarayana, N. S. (2011). Identifying the location of web objects: a study of library websites . 8th International CALIBER 2011.

Vaughan, Lewin & Shaw D. (2003). Bibliographic and Web citation, what is the difference? Journal of American Society for Information Science and Technology, 54 (14),1313-1322.

Vaughan, Liwen & Hysen, Kathy (2002). Relationship between links to journal Websites and impact factors. ASLIB Proceedings, 54(6),356-361.

Vaughan, Liwen & Tang, Juan and Du, Jian (2009). Examining the robustness of web co-link analysis. Online Information Review, 33(5), 956-972.

Vaughan, Liwen & Thelwall, Mike (2002). Scholarly use of the Web, What are the key inducers of links to journal Websites?. Journal of the American Society for Information Science and Technology, 54(1),29-38.

Vaughan, Liwen & Wu, Guozhu (2004). Links to Commercial Websites as a Source of Business Information. Scientometrics, 60(3),487-496.

Vaughan, Liwen & You, Justin (2006). Comparing business competition positions basedon Web co-link data, The global market vs. the Chinese market. Scientometrics, 68(3),611-628.

Walia, P.K. & Kaur, Prabhjeet (2008). Webometric Analysis of Associations' Websites of India. IASLIC Bulletin, 53(3),131-143.

Walia, P.K., & Kaur P. (2010). Government of India Websites, A Study. DESIDOC Journal of Library & Information Technology, 30 (4), 3-10.

Weare, C., & Lin, W. Y. (2000). Content analysis of the World Wide Web: Opportunities and challenges. Social science computer review, 18(3), 272-292.

Weber, M. (1911). "Geschaftsbericht" in verhandlungen des Ersten DeutschenSoziologietages." In Schrift der DeutschenGessellschaft fur Soziologie (pp.39-62) Vom 19-22. Oktober 1910 Frankfurt A.M,

Weber, R. P. (1990) "Basic Content Analysis". Second Edition. CA: Sage Publications.

Wilkinson, David, Thelwall, Mike, and Li, Xuemei (2003). Exploiting Hyperlinks to Study Academic Web Use. Social Science Computer Review, 21(3),340-351.

Yeravdekar, Vidya Rajiv., & Gauri Tiwari., Internationalization of Higher Education in India. New Delhi, Sage, 2017.

Yi, Kwan & Jin, Tao (2008). Hyperlink analysis of the visibility of Canadian library and information science school websites . Online Information Review, 32(3), 325- 347.

Yimin, Jiang et al. (2006). Evaluation of Cross-strait Public Library Websites. WUJNS, 11(5), p.1202-1208.

Yiping, D.; Tsunashima, F. and Ozawa, W. (2002) "The movement of agricultural journalism and farming readers after the war. Journal of Rural Economics. 74:81-85.

Zhu, Y. X.; Zhou, J.G.; Zhu, Y.X. and Zhou, J.G. (2003). "Searching coordinating and analyzing of tea literature published in China." Journal of Zhejiang University of Agriculture and Life Sciences; 29:6, 689-693.

Appendix

Format of data collection

Name of the institution:

Type of institution:

ICAR

State institution.

NGO

Private institution

Any other

Website URL :

URL domain:

Content features of the websites :

Sl.No.	Content	Tick
1	About Us	
2	Courses/Programs Offered [undergraduate / graduate / postgraduate / distance education/different trainings]	
3	Institution contacts information [Email /Phone no / Map of university and collages]	
4	Recent News	
5	Faculty contact	
6	Telephone Directory	
7	Video / Audio Ideas	
8	Tenders / Circulars	
9	Freedom of Information Act / Right To Information Act	
10	Search Features	
11	Quick Links	
12	Electronic Media	
13	Publications [University Journals / Books / Publication by Faculty]	
14	Mission	
15	Events	
16	Forth coming events	
17	Feedback	
18	Facilities / Amenities and Services	

Sl.No.	Content	Tick
19	Placement cell	
20	Jobs	
21	Departments / Infrastructure	
22	Policy	
23	Funds	
24	Awards	
25	Admission information / Application [term dates]	
26	Visitors	
27	Internal social groups / Clubs activities / student union	
28	Faculty research / Case Study	
29	Open Days	
30	Accommodation	
31	Alumni Information	
32	International [support / services]	
33	Accreditation	
34	Health service	
35	Memorandums of understanding with other universities	
36	Scholarship	
37	Library Catalogues	
38	Other information [syllabus, date sheet, revolution forms / procedure]	
39	Scholarship	
40	Students	
41	Culture and Sports	
42	Old Exam papers	
43	Exam Results	

Form of Web Content

Sl.No.	Form of Information Resources	Tick
1	Reports	
2	News Articles	
3	Statistical Data	
4	Speeches	
5	Laws and directives	
6	Contracts	
7	Maps	
8	Training Materials	

Information Domain of the Websites

Sl.No	Keywords	Tick
1	Agriculture	
2	Extension & Rural Livelihood	
3	Horticulture	
4	Forestry	
5	Animal Husbandry	
6	Sericulture	
7	Fishery	
8	Apiculture	

Languages Used in Websites

Sl.No	Languages	Tick
1	English + Bengali	
2	English	
3	English +Hindi	
4	English +Bengali+Hindi	

Thematic Areas Covered by Web Contents

Sl.No	Information of Websites	Tick
1	Agriculture	
2	Education	
3	Human Rights	
4	Market & MSME	
5	Self-Help Group & Employment	
6	Woman Empowerment	
7	Food Supply & Processing	
8	Health Care of Rural Society	
9	Field Crops &Fibres	
10	Irrigation	
11	Rural Livelihood	
12	Tribal Development	
13	Horticulture & Plantation Crops	
14	Fisheries	
15	Forest & Wildlife Conservation	
16	Animal Husbandry & Dairy	

Coverage of Intended Audience

Sl. No	Information of Websites	Tick
1	Teachers	
2	Students	
3	Parents	
4	Researchers	
5	Medium Farmers	
6	Large Farmers	
7	Employees	
8	Businessmen	
9	Small and Marginal Farmers	
10	KVK SMS	
11	Environmentalist	
12	Land Laborers	
13	Self Help Groups	
14	Joint liability Groups	
15	Women	
16	Artisans	
17	Tribal People	
18	Fishermen	

Media Forms of Websites

Sl.No	Media forms	Tick
1	Text	
2	Images	
3	Social media	
4	Video	